AI Unleashed Essentials:

The AI-Driven Leader's Quick Reference

Navigating AI: Top 100 Questions Answered
from Core Concepts to Strategic Tools

Library of congress Cataloguing-in Publication Data.

Name: Mark Kelly, author

Title: "AI Unleashed Essentials: The AI-Driven Leader's Quick
Reference"

"Navigating AI: Top 100 Questions Answered from Core
Concepts to Strategic Tools"

Description:

ISBN: 9798877984172

Subjects: Technological Innovations. / Artificial Intelligence. /
Business-Data processing

CONTENTS

Introduction

Welcome to "AI Unleashed Essentials: The AI-Driven Leader's Quick Reference," a definitive guide crafted to demystify the complexities of Artificial Intelligence (AI) and illuminate its practical applications. This book distils essential AI knowledge, complemented by real-world case studies, to equip you with a comprehensive understanding of AI, devoid of unnecessary hype. Stemming from the encouraging feedback on "AI Unleashed," particularly for the inclusion of key takeaways and practical examples, this sequel is designed to be your go-to reference, offering insightful and actionable knowledge.

As the founder of AI Ireland, I am thrilled to present this resource aimed at navigating the intricate world of AI. Whether you're a tech veteran, a business leader, or simply keen to broaden your AI knowledge, this guide is meticulously structured to deepen your understanding and enhance your practical skills in leveraging AI.

Embark on Your AI Journey:

1. **AI Basics:** Establish your journey on solid ground with a deep dive into AI's fundamental concepts and terminology, ensuring a clear understanding of the basics.

2. **AI in Business:** Transition into exploring AI's pivotal role in transforming business operations, highlighting its capacity to boost efficiency and enhance customer engagement across various industries.

3. **Ethical Considerations:** Address the critical balance between innovation and ethics, exploring the moral dilemmas AI presents and advocating for its advancement to benefit the greater good.

4. **AI Technologies:** Delve into the core technical aspects of AI, offering a comprehensive exploration of the technologies driving AI forward, including machine learning algorithms and neural networks, and their applications across sectors.

5. **Future Trends:** Peer into what the future holds for AI, examining emerging trends and the potential trajectory of AI development, with a focus on its evolving impact on society.

6. **The A-Z Appendices:** Expand your AI vocabulary with a detailed glossary of AI terminology, serving as a quick-reference guide to familiarise yourself with key terms and concepts.

7. **Real-World Case Studies:** Gain tangible insights into AI implementation through a collection of real-world case studies.

Each section, enriched with 'AI in Practice' examples and case studies, is designed for flexible navigation, allowing you to either build a comprehensive AI knowledge base or focus on areas of immediate interest or need.

Mastering AI is a marathon, not a sprint. It demands dedication, continuous learning, and strategic application. I invite you to join this journey, unlock AI's potential, and lay the foundation for innovation and success in your projects. Let this year mark a significant leap in your AI mastery, with this guide serving as an invaluable companion on your path to AI proficiency.

Mark Kelly

Founder, AI Ireland

Dublin, February 2024

AI BASICS	PAGE
Q1 What is Artificial Intelligence?	
Q2 How does AI differ from machine learning and deep learning?	
Q3 What are the main types of AI?	
Q4 What is a neural network in AI?	
Q5 How do algorithms work in AI?	
Q6 What is natural language processing (NLP)?	
Q7 What are the basic components of AI systems?	
Q8 How is AI different from human intelligence?	
Q9 What is the Turing Test in AI?	
Q10 What are the limitations of current AI technologies?	

AI BASICS	PAGE
Q11 How do AI systems learn?	
Q12 What is an AI model?	
Q13 What is data training in AI?	
Q14 How does AI use big data?	
Q15 What are the common programming languages used in AI?	
Q16 What is computer vision?	
Q17 How do AI and robotics interact?	
Q18 What is reinforcement learning in AI?	
Q19 What are expert systems in AI?	
Q20 How does AI solve problems?	

AI IN BUSINESS	PAGE
Q21 How is AI transforming business today?	
Q22 What are the key challenges businesses face in adopting AI?	
Q23 What are the benefits of AI in customer service?	
Q24 How is AI used in marketing and advertising?	
Q25 What is the role of AI in supply chain management?	
Q26 How is AI impacting financial services?	
Q27 What is AI's role in human resources?	
Q28 How can small businesses leverage AI?	
Q29 What are the risks of using AI in business?	
Q30 How does AI contribute to decision-making processes?	

ETHICAL CONSIDERATIONS	PAGE
Q51 How does the potential for AI-enhanced cyberattacks impact ethical AI development?	
Q52 How can AI contribute to or detract from societal equality?	
Q53 What role does AI play in environmental sustainability and ethical considerations therein?	
Q54 How should AI systems be designed to respect user privacy?	
Q55 What measures can ensure transparency and accountability in AI systems?	
Q56 How do ethical considerations in AI vary across cultures and regions?	
Q57 What ethical frameworks are proposed for regulating AI?	
Q58 What ethical guidelines should govern AI in sensitive sectors like healthcare and criminal justice?	
Q59 How can consumers be educated on the ethical implications of AI in products and services?	
Q60 What role do international bodies play in setting ethical standards for AI?	

AI BASICS

Introduction to Artificial Intelligence: Unveiling the Future

Quick Facts:

- **Transforming Capabilities:** AI excels in tasks once believed to be the sole domain of human intellect, such as pattern recognition, strategic planning, and creative thinking.

- **Historic Milestones:** The journey of AI began in 1955 with a checker-playing programme, marking the dawn of machine-based problem-solving.

Did You Know?

- **Origins of a Concept:** The term "Artificial Intelligence" was introduced by John McCarthy in 1956, setting the stage for a new era of research and innovation at the Dartmouth Conference.

- **Beyond Human Limits:** Modern AI systems have not only learnt but also excelled in complex games like Chess and Go, surpassing human champions and redefining competitive benchmarks.

Exploring the Essence of AI:

Artificial Intelligence, a blend of innovation and imagination, is reshaping our world. It mirrors human cognitive functions through advanced algorithms and machine learning, impacting every corner of human activity. This introductory section unfolds the essence of AI, presenting its foundational principles, key technologies, and the spectrum of its applications. From healthcare breakthroughs to smart automation in finance, AI's versatility is boundless.

Key Takeaways:

- **A Spectrum of Technologies:** AI is an umbrella term that encompasses diverse fields such as machine learning, natural language processing, and robotics, each contributing uniquely to AI's capabilities.

- **Purposeful Evolution:** The goal of AI development is multifaceted, aiming to augment human abilities, automate routine tasks, and unearth insights from data that were previously beyond reach.

- **Ethical Imperatives:** As AI becomes more woven into the fabric of society, ethical use and considerations are critical to guide its growth responsibly and ensure it serves the greater good.

Real-World Impact:

AI significantly influences our daily lives, from smartphone assistants to smart algorithms and autonomous vehicles. These technologies simplify tasks, enhance decision-making, and improve life quality, demonstrating AI's vast potential and its impact on the future.

As we wrap up this introduction and move into a detailed exploration of AI Basics, we invite you on a journey to deepen your understanding of AI. The following sections will address 20 key questions about AI, shedding light on how it works, its real-world applications, and the ethical considerations it raises.

Get ready to explore the wonders and complexities of AI as we delve into this captivating field together.

Q1. What is Artificial Intelligence?

Introduction:

Artificial Intelligence (AI) refers to the simulation of human intelligence in machines programmed to think and learn like humans.

Key Points:

- AI enables machines to perform tasks typically requiring human intelligence, including problem-solving, decision-making, and language understanding.
- It covers a broad range of technologies, from simple algorithms to complex machine learning and neural networks.

AI Insights Box:

Prognosis: AI is transforming industries by enhancing efficiency, automating tasks, and providing new insights through data analysis.

Real World Example:

Voice assistants, such as Amazon's Alexa, leverage advanced artificial intelligence (AI) technologies to interpret and respond to human speech, greatly simplifying a variety of daily tasks.[1]

Q2. How does AI differ from machine learning and deep learning?

Introduction:

AI, machine learning, and deep learning represent a hierarchy of complexity and capability in data processing and learning.

Key Points:

- AI is the broadest concept, involving machines capable of performing tasks that require human intelligence.
- Machine Learning is a subset of AI where machines learn from data without being explicitly programmed for every task.
- Deep Learning is a subset of machine learning that uses neural networks with many layers to learn from vast amounts of data.

AI Insights Box:

Prognosis: The progression from AI to deep learning signifies a move towards more autonomous, sophisticated systems capable of learning from data at a scale and depth closer to human learning.

Real World Example:

Facebook's DeepFace uses deep learning for photo tagging, achieving near-human accuracy (97.35%) in facial recognition on its social media platform.[2]

Q3. What are the main types of AI?

Introduction:

The main types of AI can be categorised based on their capabilities and functionalities.

Key Points:

- **Reactive Machines:** Basic AI systems that respond to specific inputs with specific outputs, without memory or past experience.

- **Limited Memory:** AI systems that use past experiences to inform future decisions.

- **Theory of Mind:** An advanced AI that understands emotions, beliefs, and thoughts, but is largely theoretical at this stage.

- **Self-aware AI:** Hypothetical AI that possesses its own consciousness, sensations, and emotions, far beyond current technology.

AI Insights Box:

Prognosis: As AI evolves, the move towards more advanced types like Theory of Mind and Self-aware AI promises revolutionary changes in interactions between humans and machines.

Real World Example:

Tesla's Autopilot system uses AI with Limited Memory for real-time navigation, leveraging sensors and data to make immediate driving decisions.[3]

Q4. What is a neural network in AI?

Introduction:

A neural network is a foundational technology in AI that mimics the workings of the human brain to process information.

Key Points:

- Consists of layers of nodes, or "neurons", each layer processing an aspect of the data and passing it to the next layer.
- Used in deep learning to analyse complex patterns in large datasets.

AI Insights Box:

Prognosis: Neural networks are key to advancements in AI, enabling significant breakthroughs in image and speech recognition, language translation, and more.

Real World Example:

Google's DeepMind AI assists in analysing eye scans, detecting diseases like diabetic retinopathy and macular degeneration early, improving patient outcomes.[4]

Q5. How do algorithms work in AI?

Introduction:

Algorithms in AI are sets of rules or instructions that guide the process of problem-solving and decision-making in machines.

Key Points:

- Algorithms can range from simple decision trees to complex deep learning models.
- They learn from data to make predictions or decisions without human intervention.

AI Insights Box:

Prognosis: The development of more sophisticated algorithms is crucial for the evolution of AI, enhancing its accuracy, reliability, and application areas.

Real World Example:

Netflix uses algorithms to recommend movies by analysing your viewing history, enhancing personalised content discovery.[5]

Q6. What is natural language processing (NLP)?

Introduction:

NLP is a branch of AI that enables machines to understand, interpret, and generate human language.

Key Points:

- Involves tasks such as language translation, sentiment analysis, and speech recognition.
- Uses algorithms to analyse and understand the structure and meaning of language.

AI Insights Box:

Prognosis: NLP is bridging the gap between human communication and computer understanding, with vast applications in customer service, content creation, and more.

Real World Example:

Amazon's Alexa uses NLP to understand and respond to customer queries, offering instant, voice-activated customer support.[6]

Q7. What are the basic components of AI systems?

Introduction:

AI systems are composed of several key components that enable them to function and perform tasks intelligently.

Key Points:

- **Data:** The foundation for training AI models.
- **Algorithms:** Rules and models that guide decision-making and learning.
- **Computing Power:** Hardware capable of supporting data processing and model training.
- **Interfaces:** Means for humans to interact with AI, such as APIs or voice recognition systems.

AI Insights Box:

Prognosis: The integration and advancement of these components are critical for the development of more sophisticated and efficient AI systems.

Real World Example:

Smartphones integrate CPUs, GPUs, and AI chips to enable features like Siri, offering voice-activated assistance and personalised responses.[7]

Q8. How is AI different from human intelligence?

Introduction:

AI and human intelligence differ fundamentally in their processing, learning, and problem-solving approaches.

Key Points:

- AI excels in processing and analysing large datasets quickly and accurately.
- Human intelligence is superior in emotional understanding, creativity, and adaptability.
- AI operates within predefined parameters, while humans can think abstractly and make connections between disparate concepts.

AI Insights Box:

Prognosis: The complementarity between AI and human intelligence offers immense potential for collaborative systems that leverage the strengths of both.

Real World Example:

IBM's Watson combines AI with doctors' expertise for faster, more accurate disease diagnosis, blending technology with medical insight.[8]

Q9. What is the Turing Test in AI?

Introduction:

The Turing Test, proposed by Alan Turing in 1950, is a measure of a machine's ability to exhibit intelligent behaviour indistinguishable from that of a human.

Key Points:

- Involves a human judge engaging in a natural language conversation with a machine and another human without knowing which is which.
- If the judge cannot reliably tell the machine from the human, the machine is said to have passed the test.

AI Insights Box:

Prognosis: While the Turing Test has been a foundational concept in AI, the field now also focuses on specific, practical abilities beyond mimicking human conversation.

Real World Example:

OpenAI's GPT-3 powered chatbots in customer service aim to pass the Turing Test by generating human-like responses in real-time interactions.[9]

Q10. What are the limitations of current AI technologies?

Introduction:

AI has made significant progress but faces limitations from data quality to ethical issues, affecting its effectiveness and application range.

Key Points:

- **Data Dependency:** AI's performance relies on the quality and volume of data. Poor or biased data can result in inaccuracies or amplify biases.

- **Understanding Limitations:** AI lacks the ability to comprehend context or complex concepts, limiting its capacity for tasks requiring deep understanding or empathy.

- **Ethical and Privacy Issues:** AI raises concerns about data use, privacy, and the ethical implications of its decisions, especially in areas like surveillance and employment.

- **Generalisation Challenges:** AI systems struggle to apply learned knowledge in new contexts, limiting their adaptability to unseen scenarios.

AI Insights Box:

Prognosis: Overcoming these limitations requires technological innovation and ethical frameworks to ensure AI is transparent, accountable, and aligned with human values.

Real World Example:

In the UK, autonomous vehicle tests by companies like Waymo and Oxbotica highlight AI's navigation potential. Yet, these vehicles face challenges in dynamic environments and decision-making, emphasising the need for further development in technology and ethics for public road safety.[10]

Q11. How do AI systems learn?

Introduction:

AI systems learn by analysing data, identifying patterns, and making decisions based on past experiences.

Key Points:

- **Machine Learning:** AI systems learn through machine learning by being fed large amounts of data and learning from it over time.

- **Supervised Learning:** Involves learning from a labelled dataset, where the system makes predictions and adjusts based on the accuracy of those predictions.

- **Unsupervised Learning:** The system learns to identify patterns and relationships in data without any labelled outcomes.

- **Reinforcement Learning:** AI learns through trial and error, receiving feedback from its actions to maximise a reward.

AI Insights Box:

Prognosis: The ability of AI systems to learn and improve over time is pivotal for developing more sophisticated and autonomous applications.

Real World Example:

Spotify's Discover Weekly uses AI to recommend music tracks by analysing listening habits, offering personalised playlists to users.[11]

Q12. What is an AI model?

Introduction:

An AI model is a mathematical framework that allows an AI system to make predictions or decisions based on data.

Key Points:

- AI models are built using algorithms that can learn from data.
- The model is trained using a dataset to recognise patterns and relationships.
- Once trained, it can apply its learning to new, unseen data to make predictions.

AI Insights Box:

Prognosis: AI models are at the heart of AI applications, enabling them to perform tasks ranging from simple classifications to complex problem-solving.

Real World Example:

FICO's AI models use credit histories to predict loan default risk, enhancing decision-making in lending with greater accuracy.[12]

Q13. What is data training in AI?

Introduction:

Data training in AI involves feeding data into an AI model to help it learn and make informed decisions.

Key Points:

- **Training Dataset:** A collection of data used to teach the model about the task it needs to perform.
- **Validation Dataset:** Used to tune the model's parameters and prevent overfitting.
- **Test Dataset:** Used to evaluate the model's performance on data it hasn't seen before.

AI Insights Box:

Prognosis: Effective data training is crucial for creating accurate and reliable AI models, directly impacting their success in real-world applications.

Real World Example:

Google Health's AI analyses electronic medical records to enhance diagnostic accuracy, aiding doctors in identifying diseases earlier.[13]

Q14. How does AI use big data?

Introduction:

AI uses big data to analyse and extract valuable insights from vast amounts of information, enhancing decision-making and predictions.

Key Points:

- Big data provides the raw material for AI to learn and identify patterns.

- AI algorithms process and analyse big data at speeds and scales beyond human capability.

- The combination of AI and big data is powerful, enabling advancements in personalised medicine, financial services, and more.

AI Insights Box:

Prognosis: The synergy between AI and big data is transforming how we approach complex problems, offering unprecedented opportunities for innovation.

Real World Example:

Target uses AI to analyse customer data, crafting personalised marketing strategies that improve shopping experiences and boost sales.[14]

Q15. What are the common programming languages used in AI?

Introduction:

Several programming languages are favoured in the development of AI due to their functionality and libraries.

Key Points:

- **Python:** Renowned for its simplicity and extensive libraries like TensorFlow and PyTorch.
- **R:** Preferred for statistical analysis and data visualisation.
- **Java:** Offers portability, ease of debugging, and integration with large-scale production environments.
- **C++:** Used for AI requiring high-performance computing, given its speed and efficiency.

AI Insights Box:

Prognosis: The choice of programming language can significantly affect the development and deployment of AI applications, impacting their performance and scalability.

Real World Example:

TensorFlow, developed by Google, facilitates neural network development with its extensive libraries, speeding up AI model creation and deployment.[15]

Q16. What is computer vision?

Introduction:

Computer vision is a field of AI that enables machines to interpret and understand the visual world.

Key Points:

- It involves processing and analysing digital images and videos to recognise objects, faces, and scenes.
- Uses machine learning and neural networks to mimic human visual perception.
- Applications include image recognition, autonomous vehicles, and surveillance systems.

AI Insights Box:

Prognosis: Computer vision is bridging the gap between visual data and actionable insights, with vast potential across various industries.

Real World Example:

Autonomous vehicles such as Waymo cars use computer vision for navigation.[16]

Q17. How do AI and robotics interact?

Introduction:

AI and robotics combine to create intelligent machines that can perform tasks autonomously, enhancing capabilities and efficiency.

Key Points:

- AI provides the "brain" to robots, enabling them to make decisions, learn from data, and interact with their environment.
- Robotics focuses on the physical aspect, including movement and manipulation of objects.
- Together, they enable the development of sophisticated robots that can adapt to complex tasks and environments.

AI Insights Box:

Prognosis: The integration of AI with robotics is key to the next generation of automation, offering solutions from manufacturing to healthcare.

Real World Example:

ABB's robotic arms use AI for precise manufacturing tasks, enhancing efficiency and reducing errors in industrial production lines.[17]

Q18. What is reinforcement learning in AI?

Introduction:

Reinforcement learning is an area of machine learning where an AI learns to make decisions by trial and error, maximising some notion of cumulative reward.

Key Points:

- It involves an agent that interacts with its environment, receives feedback in the form of rewards or penalties, and learns the best actions to take.

- Used in complex decision-making scenarios where explicit programming is not feasible.

- Applications include game playing, robotics, and optimisation problems.

AI Insights Box:

Prognosis: Reinforcement learning is advancing AI's decision-making capabilities, pushing the boundaries of autonomy and efficiency.

Real World Example:

DeepMind's AlphaGo uses reinforcement learning to master strategies in games like Go, demonstrating AI's ability to learn and outperform human experts.[18]

Q19. What are expert systems in AI?

Introduction:

Expert systems are AI applications designed to solve complex problems by mimicking the decision-making ability of a human expert.

Key Points:

- They use a knowledge base and a set of rules to analyse information and make conclusions.
- Primarily used in fields where decision-making is critical, such as medicine, engineering, and finance.
- Expert systems can explain their reasoning and conclusions, providing valuable insights.

AI Insights Box:

Prognosis: While expert systems represent early AI, their ability to replicate expert human decision-making continues to be valuable in specific domains.

Real World Example:

Microsoft's Project Hanover uses AI to diagnose cancers more accurately by analysing medical data and research papers, aiding in personalized treatment plans.[19]

Q20. How does AI solve problems?

Introduction:

AI solves problems by processing vast amounts of data, learning from experiences, and applying learned knowledge to new situations.

Key Points:

- AI uses algorithms and models to analyse data, identify patterns, and predict outcomes.
- Machine learning and deep learning enable AI to improve its problem-solving over time.
- AI's problem-solving capabilities are applied across various fields, from healthcare diagnostics to financial forecasting.

AI Insights Box:

Prognosis: AI's problem-solving abilities are revolutionising industries, making processes more efficient, accurate, and cost-effective.

Real World Example:

Salesforce uses AI in its CRM platform to predict consumer trends, enabling businesses to tailor their marketing strategies for targeted outreach.[20]

Footnotes

1) Learn more about how Alexa, Amazon's voice assistant, is transforming interactions with technology here: https://developer.amazon.com/en-US/alexa#:~:text=What%20Is%20Alexa%3F,technology%20they%20use%20every%20day](https://developer.amazon.com/en-US/alexa#:~:text=What%20Is%20Alexa%3F,technology%20they%20use%20every%20day)

2) Explore further about Facebook's DeepFace technology and its applications in facial recognition here: https://research.facebook.com/publications/deepface-closing-the-gap-to-human-level-performance-in-face-verification/

3) Discover more about Tesla's Autopilot system and its integration of AI for real-time navigation here: https://www.tesla.com/support/autopilot

4) Learn more about how Google's DeepMind AI contributes to early disease detection in eye scans here: https://www.technologyreview.com/2019/04/01/136256/deepmind-has-made-a-prototype-product-that-can-diagnose-eye-diseases/

5) Find out more about how Netflix uses algorithms for personalised content recommendations based on user viewing history here: https://research.netflix.com/research-area/recommendations

6) Explore further about how Amazon's Alexa utilises Natural Language Processing (NLP) for voice-activated customer support here: https://developer.amazon.com/fr-FR/alexa/alexa-skills-kit/nlu

7) Discover more about the integration of CPUs, GPUs, and AI chips in smartphones for features like voice-activated assistance here: https://www.qualcomm.com/products/technology/artificial-intelligence/what-is-ai-faq/how-do-phones-use-ai

8) Learn more about how IBM's Watson integrates AI with medical expertise for disease diagnosis here: https://www.ibm.com/watson

9) Find out more about OpenAI's GPT-3 powered chatbots and their goal of passing the Turing Test with human-like responses here: https://gpt3demo.com/apps/giving-gpt-3-a-turing-test

10) Learn more about the challenges and advancements in autonomous vehicle technology, particularly in navigation and real-world driving conditions here: https://link.springer.com/article/10.1007/s40534-016-0117-3

11) Explore further about Spotify's Discover Weekly and how it uses AI for personalised music recommendations here: https://medium.com/the-sound-of-ai/spotifys-discover-weekly-explained-breaking-from-your-music-bubble-or-maybe-not-b506da144123

12) Discover more about how FICO's AI models predict loan default risk using credit histories here: https://www.fico.com/en/products/fico-responsible-ai

13) Learn more about how Google Health's AI enhances diagnostic accuracy in medical records analysis here: https://health.google/health-research/

14) Find out more about how Target uses AI for personalized marketing strategies based on customer data here: https://targetai.ai/en

15) Explore further about TensorFlow and its role in neural network development here: https://www.tensorflow.org/about/case-studies

16) Discover more about how autonomous vehicles like Waymo cars use computer vision for navigation here: https://support.google.com/waymo/answer/9190838?hl=en

17) Learn more about how ABB's robotic arms use AI for precise manufacturing tasks here: https://new.abb.com/news/detail/102366/prsrl-abbs-ai-enabled-robotic-item-picker-makes-fulfilment-faster-and-more-efficient

18) Find out more about DeepMind's AlphaGo and its use of reinforcement learning in mastering games like Go here: https://deepmind.google/technologies/alphago/

19) Explore further about Microsoft's Project Hanover and its use of AI in cancer diagnosis here:

https://www.microsoft.com/en-us/research/group/real-world-evidence/

20) Discover more about how Salesforce uses AI in its CRM platform for predicting consumer trends here: https://medium.com/@forcedigest.com/the-role-of-salesforce-ai-in-predictive-analytics-and-decision-making-c074460da5bc

AI IN BUSINESS

Introduction to Artificial Intelligence in Business

Diving deeper into the core principles of AI, this section launches us into a comprehensive analysis of Artificial Intelligence's critical impact on the business world, expressed through 20 thought-provoking questions.

Q21. How is AI transforming business today?

Introduction:

AI is revolutionising business practices, streamlining operations, and offering unprecedented insights and efficiencies.

Key Points:

- **Task Automation:** AI simplifies operations, automating routine tasks to allow employees to focus on strategic areas.

- **Data-Driven Insights:** Utilises sophisticated data analysis to uncover critical insights, improving decision-making.

- **Customer Experience:** Enhances customer engagement with personalised services and support, meeting unique needs.

AI Insights Box:

Prognosis: AI's integration into business transcends mere efficiency; it's a strategic tool for outpacing competition, driving growth, and sparking innovation.

Real World Example:

In the retail sector, AI plays a pivotal role. For instance, companies like ASOS, a global online fashion retailer, utilise AI for supply chain optimisation, market trend forecasting, and personalised shopping experiences. ASOS employs AI algorithms to manage inventory efficiently and tailor marketing efforts, resulting in increased sales and heightened customer satisfaction.[1]

Q22. What are the key challenges businesses face in adopting AI?

Introduction:

Despite its potential, businesses encounter several hurdles in integrating AI into their operations.

Key Points:

- **Data Quality and Quantity:** Access to high-quality, large-scale data is critical for effective AI.
- **Skill Gaps:** A shortage of AI expertise can hinder implementation.
- **Cost:** Initial investment and maintenance of AI systems can be significant.
- **Ethical and Privacy Concerns:** Businesses must navigate the ethical implications and privacy concerns associated with AI.

AI Insights Box:

Prognosis: Addressing these challenges is crucial for businesses to fully leverage AI's potential while maintaining trust and integrity.

Real World Example:

The University of Oxford's "AI for Everyone" initiative offers industry-focused AI training, addressing the skill gap in various sectors.[2]

Q23. What are the benefits of AI in customer service?

Introduction:

AI is transforming customer service, offering benefits that significantly enhance the customer experience.

Key Points:

- **24/7 Availability:** AI systems, like chatbots, provide round-the-clock support.

- **Personalisation:** AI can tailor interactions based on customer data, offering relevant solutions and recommendations.

- **Efficiency:** Handles large volumes of queries simultaneously, reducing wait times.

AI Insights Box:

Prognosis: AI is setting new standards in customer service, driving satisfaction and loyalty through personalised, efficient interactions.

Real World Example:

British Telecom (BT) uses AI-powered chatbots like "Billie" to swiftly handle customer inquiries, reducing response times and improving customer support.[3]

Q24. How is AI used in marketing and advertising?

Introduction:

AI is reshaping marketing and advertising strategies with its ability to analyse data and automate decision-making.

Key Points:

- **Targeted Advertising:** AI algorithms can target ads based on user behaviour and preferences.
- **Content Generation:** AI tools generate personalised content for different segments of the audience.
- **ROI Optimisation:** AI analyses campaigns in real-time, adjusting strategies for maximum return on investment.

AI Insights Box:

Prognosis: AI in marketing and advertising enhances engagement, conversion rates, and ROI, making campaigns more effective and data-driven.

Real World Example:

AI-driven programmatic advertising, as seen in platforms like Criteo, uses real-time data analysis to place highly relevant ads for users. This approach boosts engagement and results in higher click-through rates and ROI for advertisers.[4]

Q25. What is the role of AI in supply chain management?

Introduction:

AI is a game-changer in supply chain management, enhancing efficiency, visibility, and responsiveness.

Key Points:

- **Demand Forecasting:** AI predicts market demand, allowing for better stock management.
- **Logistics Optimisation:** Enhances route planning and reduces delivery times.
- **Supplier Selection:** AI evaluates suppliers based on reliability and cost, improving procurement strategies.

AI Insights Box:

Prognosis: AI's impact on supply chains is transformative, enabling smarter, more resilient operations that can adapt to changing market conditions.

Real World Example:

Zara uses AI to optimise its supply chain and fashion forecasting. Analysing customer preferences, sales data, and fashion trends, Zara's AI algorithms predict future fashion trends, enabling rapid production adjustments and reducing inventory waste, thus enhancing market responsiveness and sustainability.[5]

Q26. How is AI impacting financial services?

Introduction:

AI is significantly influencing financial services, from enhancing customer experiences to improving risk management.

Key Points:

- **Fraud Detection:** AI systems identify suspicious activities in real-time, reducing fraud.
- **Algorithmic Trading:** AI analyses market data to make trading decisions faster than humanly possible.
- **Personal Financial Management:** AI offers personalised investment and savings advice to customers.

AI Insights Box:

Prognosis: AI is reshaping financial services, offering more secure, efficient, and personalised experiences for customers.

Real World Example:

PayPal uses AI to monitor for unusual account activity, effectively preventing fraud. By analysing transaction patterns, the system quickly identifies anomalies, triggering alerts and preemptive actions to safeguard accounts against unauthorised access and fraudulent transactions.[6]

Q27. What is AI's role in human resources?

Introduction:

AI is transforming HR practices, making them more efficient and data-driven.

Key Points:

- **Recruitment Automation:** AI screens resumes and identifies the most suitable candidates.
- **Employee Engagement:** Analyses employee feedback and performance data to improve satisfaction and productivity.
- **Training and Development:** Personalises learning and development programs based on individual employee needs.

AI Insights Box:

Prognosis: AI in HR not only streamlines administrative tasks but also enhances employee engagement and development strategies.

Real World Example:

UPS utilises AI and machine learning to optimize delivery routes, improving efficiency and reducing fuel consumption. By analysing traffic patterns, weather data, and package delivery constraints, UPS's algorithms design the most efficient routes, enhancing on-time delivery rates and minimizing environmental impact.[7]

Q28. How can small businesses leverage AI?

Introduction:

Small businesses can utilise AI to compete more effectively, streamline operations, and enhance customer experiences.

Key Points:

- **Customer Insights:** AI tools analyse customer data to inform marketing and sales strategies.
- **Operational Efficiency:** Automates routine tasks, allowing small business owners to focus on strategic growth.
- **Product and Service Innovation:** AI identifies trends and opportunities for new offerings.

AI Insights Box:

Prognosis: AI offers small businesses powerful tools to optimise operations, understand customers better, and innovate, leveling the playing field with larger competitors.

Real World Example:

Etsy, an e-commerce platform for handmade and vintage items, leverages AI to personalise the online shopping experience for its vast community of buyers and sellers. By utilising AI algorithms to analyse user preferences, search history, and purchase behaviour, Etsy provides customised product recommendations and search results. This not only enhances the user experience by making product discovery more relevant and engaging but also supports small retailers in effectively reaching their target audience, showcasing how AI can empower small businesses to compete in the digital marketplace.[8]

Q29. What are the risks of using AI in business?

Introduction:

While AI presents numerous opportunities, it also poses risks that businesses need to manage.

Key Points:

- **Bias and Fairness:** AI systems can perpetuate biases present in their training data.
- **Job Displacement:** Automation may lead to the displacement of certain job categories.
- **Security Risks:** AI systems can be targeted by cyber-attacks, posing data security risks.
- **Dependence:** Overreliance on AI could impact decision-making and innovation.

AI Insights Box:

Prognosis: Businesses need to address these risks through ethical AI practices, continuous monitoring, and balancing AI with human oversight.

Real World Example:

Google's Project Euphonia trains AI on diverse speech patterns, including those with impairments, to enhance voice recognition accessibility, demonstrating a commitment to inclusivity and reducing bias in AI technologies.[9]

Q30. How does AI contribute to decision-making processes?

Introduction:

AI enhances decision-making by providing data-driven insights, predictive analysis, and automating routine decisions.

Key Points:

- **Data Processing:** AI can process and analyse vast amounts of data quickly, uncovering insights not readily apparent to humans.

- **Predictive Analytics:** Forecasts future trends, helping businesses prepare and adapt.

- **Automated Decision-Making:** For routine decisions, AI can automate the process, ensuring efficiency and consistency.

AI Insights Box:

Prognosis: AI's role in decision-making is increasingly central, offering the potential to significantly improve outcomes by leveraging deep insights and automating processes.

Real World Example:

Walmart uses AI to fine-tune inventory, analysing sales, weather, and buying trends to ensure the right stock levels. This reduces waste and boosts sales, improving efficiency and sustainability by keeping essential items available.[10]

Q31. What are predictive analytics in AI?

Introduction:

Predictive analytics in AI involves using data, statistical algorithms, and machine learning techniques to identify the likelihood of future outcomes based on historical data.

Key Points:

- **Forecasting:** AI analyses patterns in data to predict future trends.

- **Risk Assessment:** Helps in evaluating risks in various scenarios, from credit risk to supply chain disruptions.

- **Personalisation:** Enables tailored recommendations and services by anticipating customer preferences.

AI Insights Box:

Prognosis: The use of predictive analytics is expanding, offering businesses critical insights for strategic planning, risk management, and enhanced customer engagement.

Real World Example:

Amazon leverages AI for predictive analytics, analysing customer data to forecast buying behaviors and personalise recommendations, enhancing the shopping experience and boosting sales and loyalty. This demonstrates AI's impact on online retail with targeted engagement strategies.[11]

Q32. How is AI used in e-commerce?

Introduction:

AI is revolutionising business practices through automation, data-driven insights, and enhanced customer interactions.

Key Points:

- **Task Automation:** AI simplifies operations, automating routine tasks to allow employees to focus on strategic areas.
- **Data-Driven Insights:** Utilises sophisticated data analysis to uncover critical insights, improving decision-making.
- **Customer Experience:** Enhances customer engagement with personalised services and support, meeting unique needs.

AI Insights Box:

Prognosis: AI's integration into business transcends mere efficiency; it's a strategic tool for outpacing competition, driving growth, and sparking innovation.

Real World Example:

Siemens employs AI for predictive maintenance, using sensors and analytics to foresee equipment failures, thus cutting downtime and costs. This approach enhances efficiency and exemplifies AI's role in revolutionising manufacturing, demonstrating how AI boosts productivity and cost savings.[12]

Q33. What are the ethical considerations for businesses using AI?

Introduction:

The deployment of AI within businesses brings to the forefront crucial ethical considerations that necessitate careful and responsible management.

Key Points:

- **Bias and Fairness:** It is imperative to design AI systems that neither inherit existing biases nor introduce new prejudices.

- **Transparency and Explainability:** Making AI decisions clear and comprehensible for all stakeholders is essential for accountability.

- **Privacy:** The confidentiality of customer and employee information processed by AI must be rigorously safeguarded.

AI Insights Box:

Prognosis: Adhering to ethical AI practices is fundamental for cultivating trust and guaranteeing the technology's responsible and sustainable application in the commercial realm.

Real World Example:

IBM's AI Fairness 360 toolkit is a real-world initiative aimed at improving fairness in AI models. It provides developers and businesses with the means to test and mitigate bias in their AI systems, ensuring more equitable and transparent decision-making processes.[13]

Q34. How does AI impact employment in various sectors?

Introduction:

The impact of AI on employment is complex, presenting a mix of job transformation, creation, and displacement across different sectors.

Key Points:

- **Job Transformation:** AI automates routine tasks, shifting the focus of jobs towards more complex and value-added activities.

- **Job Creation:** The advent of new technologies leads to the emergence of novel job roles in AI development, management, and ethical oversight.

- **Job Displacement:** Roles centred around repetitive or manual tasks face the highest risk of automation.

AI Insights Box:

Prognosis: The integration of AI into the workforce represents both challenges and opportunities, underscoring the importance of skills development and adaptability.

Real World Example:

Amazon's use of AI and robotics in its fulfilment centres serves as a notable example. While automating various warehousing tasks, the company has simultaneously created thousands of new jobs in robot maintenance, AI system development, and logistics management, showcasing a direct impact on employment dynamics in the retail and logistics sector.[14]

Q35. What is AI's role in product development?

Introduction:

AI significantly enhances product development processes, from initial concept to market launch, by fostering innovation, streamlining design phases, and offering bespoke solutions.

Key Points:

- **Market Analysis:** Utilises AI algorithms to sift through market data and customer feedback, pinpointing potential product opportunities.

- **Design and Prototyping:** Employs AI-powered tools to expedite the design phase and facilitate swift prototyping, making iteration faster and more cost-effective.

- **Personalisation:** Leverages AI to customise products, ensuring they align with specific customer desires and preferences, thereby increasing satisfaction and loyalty.

AI Insights Box:

Prognosis: AI stands as a pivotal force in product development, equipping businesses with the tools to more accurately and efficiently address market needs and stay ahead of industry trends.

Real World Example:

Nike's use of AI in creating the Adapt BB basketball shoes showcases a real-world application. By analysing vast amounts of data on athlete movement, Nike used AI to design shoes that can automatically adjust their fit to the wearer's foot, providing personalised comfort and support. This innovation not only highlights AI's role in product personalisation but also in enhancing athletic performance through smart wearables.[15]

Q36. How is AI used in data security and fraud detection?

Introduction:

AI is revolutionising data security and fraud detection, employing advanced technologies to scrutinise patterns and pinpoint irregularities, thereby enhancing protective measures.

Key Points:

- **Real-Time Monitoring:** AI technologies scrutinise transactions and user behaviour around the clock, swiftly identifying any suspicious activity.

- **Anomaly Detection:** By recognising deviations from established norms, AI signals potential fraud or security lapses.

- **Predictive Analysis:** AI anticipates possible security threats and instances of fraud, facilitating pre-emptive action.

AI Insights Box:

Prognosis: AI is markedly enhancing the security domain, bolstering system defences against cyber-attacks and fraudulent activities.

Real World Example:

Mastercard's Decision Intelligence technology uses AI to improve data security and fraud detection by analysing transactions in real time to assess fraud risk, leading to fewer false declines and a better customer experience.[16]

Q37. What are the implications of AI in corporate governance?

Introduction:

AI is reshaping corporate governance, introducing sophisticated tools that enhance decision-making, risk management, and regulatory compliance.

Key Points:

- **Decision Support:** AI equips leaders with analytical insights, guiding strategic decisions through data-driven evidence.
- **Risk Management:** AI improves the detection and evaluation of corporate risks, offering advanced predictive capabilities.
- **Compliance Monitoring:** AI streamlines the oversight of regulatory compliance, significantly mitigating the risk of infractions.

AI Insights Box:

Prognosis: Integrating AI into governance frameworks promises increased operational efficiency, greater transparency, and improved compliance adherence, necessitating mindful ethical oversight.

Real World Example:

Deloitte's AI-driven "Regulatory Compliance" tools automate compliance monitoring with laws like GDPR, using natural language processing and machine learning to efficiently spot and address potential issues.[17]

Q38. How does AI affect customer privacy?

Introduction:

AI's role in refining customer service also brings to light significant privacy and data protection concerns.

Key Points:

- **Data Collection:** The need for extensive data by AI systems prompts critical discussions about user consent and the principle of data minimisation.

- **Surveillance:** The augmented use of AI for monitoring activities can encroach on individual privacy, leading to concerns over intrusive surveillance.

- **Data Security:** The accumulation and processing of vast datasets by AI systems amplify the risks associated with data breaches.

AI Insights Box:

Prognosis: Achieving a harmonious balance between AI advancements and the safeguarding of privacy rights is crucial for sustaining consumer confidence and adhering to stringent data protection regulations.

Real World Example:

Apple's approach to AI in its products, such as the iPhone, demonstrates a commitment to privacy by design. The company integrates AI features, like facial recognition and Siri, in ways that process data on the device itself rather than transmitting personal information to the cloud. This method not only enhances functionality but also aligns with privacy principles, ensuring user data remains secure and minimising the risk of breaches.[18]

Q39. What is the Future of AI in Business?

Introduction:

The trajectory of AI in business forecasts a shift towards more sophisticated, intelligent, and groundbreaking applications spanning all industries.

Key Points:

- **Augmented Workforce:** AI is set to collaborate closely with humans, augmenting skills and boosting productivity.
- **Customised Experiences:** Companies will harness AI to deliver personalisation at levels never seen before.
- **Sustainable Operations:** AI will propel operational efficiencies, cutting waste and championing eco-friendly practices.

AI Insights Box:

Prognosis: AI is on course to become a fundamental element in future business strategies, catalysing expansion, innovation, and ecological sustainability.

Real World Example:

Starbucks' use of AI in their Deep Brew platform exemplifies the future of AI in business. This AI-driven initiative enhances customer service by personalising order suggestions at their drive-thrus, optimising staff scheduling, and managing inventory more efficiently. By analysing customer preferences and store data, Starbucks delivers tailor-made experiences, showcasing how AI can drive both customer satisfaction and operational excellence.[19]

Q40. How Can Businesses Stay Updated with AI Advancements?

Introduction:

To maintain competitiveness and foster innovation, businesses must stay abreast of rapid AI advancements.

Key Points:

- **Continuous Learning:** Promote perpetual education and skill development in AI among staff.

- **Collaboration:** Forge partnerships with academic entities, tech companies, and AI research communities.

- **Innovation Labs:** Create specialised teams or divisions focused on investigating AI technologies and conducting pilot projects.

- **Industry Events:** Actively participate in AI-related conferences, webinars, and workshops to gain insights and network.

AI Insights Box:

Prognosis: Keeping updated and flexible is essential for effectively capitalising on AI advancements, allowing businesses to fully exploit the technology's capabilities.

Real World Example:

Google's collaboration with DeepMind showcases strategic AI innovation, enhancing healthcare analytics and data center efficiency, setting a benchmark for AI integration in business and driving significant improvements across sectors.[20]

Footnotes

1) Explore further about the role of AI in the retail sector, including its applications in supply chain optimisation and personalised shopping experiences here: https://journals.bilpubgroup.com/index.php/jcsr/article/view/1591

   Discover more about the University of Oxford's "AI for Everyone" initiative and its contributions to addressing the skill gap in various sectors through industry-focused AI training here: https://www.oxai.org/

2) Learn more about British Telecom (BT) and its use of AI-powered chatbots like "Billie" to enhance customer support by swiftly handling inquiries here: https://www.verdict.co.uk/ai-chatbots-will-soon-be-able-to-make-business-process-suggestions-says-bt-cdo-kevin-lee/?cf-view

3) Find out more about AI-driven programmatic advertising, as seen in platforms like Criteo, and its use of real-time data analysis to place highly relevant ads for users, resulting in increased engagement and ROI for advertisers here: https://www.criteo.com/technology/ai-engine/

4) Explore further about how Zara utilises AI to optimise its supply chain and fashion forecasting, enhancing market responsiveness and sustainability through rapid production adjustments and reduced inventory waste based on predicted

fashion trends here: https://www.linkedin.com/pulse/zaras-just-in-telligent-supply-chain-sanish-mathews/

5) Discover more about PayPal's use of AI to monitor for unusual account activity and prevent fraud by quickly identifying anomalies in transaction patterns here: https://www.paypal.com/us/brc/article/paypal-machine-learning-stop-fraud

6) Discover more about UPS's use of AI and machine learning to optimise delivery routes, improving efficiency and reducing environmental impact through the design of the most efficient routes based on traffic patterns, weather data, and package delivery constraints here: https://www.linkedin.com/pulse/ai-powered-logistics-benefits-automated-route-planning-wize-digital-oeusf/

7) Find out more about Etsy's utilization of AI to personalise the online shopping experience for its community of buyers and sellers, enhancing product discovery and supporting small retailers in reaching their target audience here: https://www.insiderintelligence.com/content/how-shopify-ebay-etsy-use-ai-strengthen-seller-relationships-customer-experience

8) Learn more about Google's Project Euphonia and its training of AI on diverse speech patterns, including those with impairments, to enhance voice recognition accessibility and reduce bias in AI technologies, showcasing a commitment to inclusivity in AI development here: https://sites.research.google/euphonia/about/

9) Discover more about Walmart's use of AI-driven analytics for inventory management, optimising stock levels, and minimising waste while maximising sales opportunities across its global stores and online platforms here: https://tech.walmart.com/content/walmart-global-tech/en_us/news/articles/walmarts-ai-powered-inventory-system-brightens-the-holidays.html

10) Learn more about Amazon's use of AI for predictive analytics in transforming online retail through personalised recommendations and discounts based on customer data here: https://www.forbes.com/sites/amazonwebservices/2021/12/03/predicting-the-future-of-demand-how-amazon-is-reinventing-forecasting-with-machine-learning/?sh=70e0481b1b6b

11) Find out more about Siemens' implementation of AI-driven predictive maintenance in manufacturing operations, reducing downtime and maintenance costs through proactive equipment failure prediction here: https://www.siemens.com/global/en/products/services/digital-enterprise-services/analytics-artificial-intelligence-services/predictive-services.html

12) Explore further about IBM's AI Fairness 360 toolkit and its real-world initiative aimed at improving fairness in AI models by providing developers and businesses with means to test and mitigate bias here: https://www.ibm.com/opensource/open/projects/ai-fairness-360/

13) Discover more about Amazon's use of AI and robotics in its fulfilment centres, showcasing its impact on employment dynamics in the retail and logistics sector here: https://www.aboutamazon.com/news/operations/how-amazon-deploys-robots-in-its-operations-facilities

14) Learn more about Nike's use of AI in product personalization, such as the Adapt BB basketball shoes, and its role in enhancing athletic performance through smart wearables here: https://www.linkedin.com/pulse/how-nike-leverages-ai-exceptional-customer-experience-sparkouttech/

15) Find out more about Mastercard's Decision Intelligence technology and its application in enhancing data security and fraud detection through real-time transaction analysis here: https://www.mastercard.com/globalrisk/en/resources/all-resources/detect.html

16) Explore further about Deloitte's "Regulatory Compliance" AI solutions and their impact on corporate governance by automating and enhancing compliance monitoring with global data protection laws here: https://www2.deloitte.com/be/en/blog/digital-strategic-risk/2023/harnessing-generative-ai-regulatory-compliance.html

17) Discover more about Apple's approach to AI in its products, prioritizing privacy by design and processing data on the device itself for enhanced functionality and user data security here: https://www.apple.com/privacy/docs/A_Day_in_the_Life_of_Your_Data.pdf

18) Learn more about Starbucks' use of AI in their Deep Brew platform for personalised customer experiences and operational excellence through staff scheduling and inventory management here: https://stories.starbucks.com/stories/2020/how-starbucks-plans-to-use-technology-to-nurture-the-human-spirit/

19) Find out more about Google's partnership with DeepMind and its impact on AI innovation across various domains, from healthcare analytics to energy efficiency in data centres here: https://deepmind.google/about/

Ethical Considerations and Regulatory Frameworks in AI

Introduction:

Transitioning from our deep dive into AI in Business, we arrive at the crucial third part of our exploration: "Ethical Considerations and AI Regulation." This segment is dedicated to unraveling the intricate web of moral dilemmas and regulatory challenges that accompany the advancement of artificial intelligence. As we navigate through this pivotal area, we aim to address the top 20 questions that highlight the pressing need for responsible AI development and use. Our journey here is not just about understanding AI's potential but also about ensuring that its integration across various sectors is conducted with a keen awareness of ethical standards and legal frameworks. This part of the book seeks to shed light on how we can harness AI's power while safeguarding our societal values and promoting a regulatory environment that supports innovation without compromising on accountability and fairness.

Q41. What are the Ethical Concerns Associated with AI?

Introduction:

As AI increasingly makes decisions traditionally handled by humans, it introduces complex ethical dilemmas that challenge our societal norms and values.

Key Points:

- **Autonomy vs Control:** Balancing AI's decision-making autonomy with human oversight to prevent harm.
- **Bias and Fairness:** Ensuring AI systems do not perpetuate or amplify societal biases.
- **Accountability:** Determining who is responsible when AI decisions lead to negative outcomes.

AI Insights Box:

Prognosis: Ethical frameworks and rigorous testing are essential to navigate the dilemmas AI presents, aiming to harness its benefits while minimising potential harms.

Real World Example:

HSBC employs AI in loan approval processes, actively working to mitigate algorithmic bias to ensure fair and ethical decision-making in lending practices.[1]

Q42. How can bias in AI algorithms be identified and mitigated?

Introduction:

Identifying and mitigating bias in AI algorithms is crucial for ensuring fairness and equity in AI-driven decisions.

Key Points:

- **Data Analysis:** Examining the data sets for biases that could skew AI decisions.
- **Algorithmic Transparency:** Making the AI decision-making process understandable and reviewable.
- **Diverse Testing:** Using diverse groups to test AI systems before deployment.

AI Insights Box:

Prognosis: Ongoing vigilance and diverse input are key to reducing bias in AI, promoting fairness and trust in technology.

Real World Example:

Google's TensorFlow Fairness Indicators offer a toolkit for evaluating and improving algorithmic fairness, helping developers identify and mitigate bias in AI models before deployment.[2]

Q43. What are the ethical considerations in deploying AI for surveillance?

Introduction:

The use of AI in surveillance raises significant ethical considerations, balancing public safety with individual privacy rights.

Key Points:

- **Privacy:** Insuring surveillance AI respects individual privacy and complies with data protection laws.
- **Consent:** Navigating the complexities of consent in public and semi-public spaces.
- **Proportionality:** Assessing whether the surveillance use is proportionate to the intended benefits.

AI Insights Box:

Prognosis: Ethical deployment of AI in surveillance requires transparent policies, strict regulatory compliance, and public dialogue to maintain societal trust.

Real World Example:

London utilises AI-enhanced CCTV within its surveillance systems, carefully balancing ethical considerations to protect privacy while boosting public safety measures.[3]

Q44. How does AI impact data privacy and individual consent?

Introduction:

AI's capacity to process vast amounts of personal data has profound implications for data privacy and the notion of consent.

Key Points:

- **Data Collection:** The extensive collection of data by AI systems challenges traditional consent mechanisms.
- **Informed Consent:** Ensuring individuals understand how their data will be used by AI.
- **Privacy Protection:** Implementing robust data protection measures to safeguard personal information.

AI Insights Box:

Prognosis: Strengthening data protection frameworks and enhancing transparency around AI data use are critical for safeguarding privacy in the AI era.

Real World Example:

Mayo Clinic employs AI to analyse patient data, emphasising stringent consent processes and robust data protection measures to safeguard patient privacy.[4]

Q45. What responsibilities do AI developers have in ensuring ethical use of AI?

Introduction:

AI developers play a pivotal role in ensuring the ethical development and deployment of AI technologies.

Key Points:

- **Ethical design:** Incorporating ethical considerations into the design phase of AI development.

- **Transparency:** Making AI algorithms and their decision-making processes accessible and understandable.

- **Impact Assessment:** Conducting thorough assessments of potential social and ethical impacts before deployment.

AI Insights Box:

Prognosis: Developers are the frontline guardians of ethical AI, responsible for embedding ethical principles into AI systems from inception to deployment.

Real World Example:

IBM, Amazon, and Microsoft halted or restricted their facial recognition technologies, addressing privacy, bias, and surveillance concerns, advocating for ethical AI use and stronger regulations to protect human rights.[5]

Q46. How can ethical AI be promoted in competitive business environments?

Introduction:

Promoting ethical AI in competitive business environments requires balancing innovation with responsibility, ensuring that ethical practices contribute to a company's competitive advantage.

Key Points:

- **Corporate Ethics Programs:** Integrating AI ethics into corporate governance and decision-making processes.
- **Collaboration and Sharing:** Encouraging industry-wide collaborations to set and uphold ethical standards.
- **Market Differentiation:** Using ethical AI practices as a point of differentiation, appealing to increasingly ethically conscious consumers.

AI Insights Box:

Prognosis: Ethical AI can become a competitive edge, with businesses that prioritise responsible AI practices gaining trust and loyalty from customers and partners.

Real World Example:

Microsoft has developed comprehensive ethical AI guidelines, distinguishing itself in the market by attracting customers who prioritize data privacy and fairness in technology.[6]

Q47. What are the long-term ethical implications of autonomous AI systems?

Introduction:

The long-term ethical implications of autonomous AI systems encompass a broad range of societal, legal, and existential considerations, challenging our conventional understanding of agency, responsibility, and ethics.

Key Points:

- **Autonomy and Control:** Balancing the benefits of AI autonomy with necessary human oversight to prevent unforeseen consequences.
- **Societal Impact:** Assessing the long-term effects on employment, social interactions, and human behavior.
- **Existential Risks:** Considering the potential for highly autonomous AI systems to pose risks to humanity under certain scenarios.

AI Insights Box:

Prognosis: Addressing the long-term ethical implications requires proactive governance, ongoing research, and a global dialogue on the future role of AI in society.

Real World Example:

Global initiatives like the Asilomar AI Principles guide the ethical development of autonomous systems, focusing on safety and societal well-being.[7]

Q48. What are the current regulation trends around AI worldwide?

Introduction:

Global AI regulatory trends prioritise ethical use, data privacy, transparency, and accountability. Efforts are underway globally to create frameworks that balance innovation with societal safeguards and ethical considerations.

Key Points:

- **Global Collaboration:** Standardisation of AI regulations through initiatives like the OECD's AI Principles and the G7's guidelines.

- **Regional Regulations:** The EU's comprehensive AI Act leads, with varied approaches in other regions.

- **Sector-Specific Focus:** Enhanced regulatory attention on AI in healthcare, finance, and autonomous vehicles.

- **Ethics and Data Governance:** A focus on ethical AI development and strict data protection, especially under the GDPR in Europe.

AI Insights Box:

Prognosis: The direction of AI regulation is towards more unified, ethical, and globally interoperable frameworks. The focus is likely to shift towards standardising AI practices and addressing the challenges posed by emerging technologies such as deepfakes and autonomous decision-making systems.

Real-World Example:

The European Union's proposed AI Act is set to become one of the first comprehensive legal frameworks for AI globally. It categorises AI systems by risk, enforcing stringent requirements on high-risk applications. This act is a significant step towards ethical, transparent AI use, respecting fundamental rights and possibly serving as a benchmark for worldwide regulation.[8]

Q49. How do regulations like the EU AI Act aim to address ethical concerns in AI?

Introduction:

The EU AI Act represents a comprehensive regulatory approach to mitigate ethical concerns in AI, aiming to safeguard fundamental rights while fostering innovation within the European Union.

Key Points:

- **Risk-Based Approach:** Categorising AI systems according to their risk levels to determine the regulatory requirements.

- **Transparency Obligations:** Mandating clear information on AI's workings for users, ensuring informed consent.

- **Accountability and Governance:** Establishing strict accountability measures for AI developers and operators, including conformity assessments and post-market monitoring.

AI Insights Box:

Prognosis: The EU AI Act serves as a pioneering model for global AI governance, balancing ethical considerations with the need for technological advancement.

Real World Example:

The EU's AI Act imposes strict requirements on high-risk AI systems in healthcare, focusing on ensuring patient safety and data privacy across member states.[9]

Q50. What ethical challenges are unique to generative AI technologies?

Introduction:

Generative AI technologies, such as GPT and DALL-E, pose unique ethical challenges, particularly around content creation, intellectual property, and authenticity.

Key Points:

- **Content Authenticity:** Distinguishing between human-generated and AI-generated content.
- **Intellectual Property Rights:** Addressing the ownership and copyright of AI-generated works.
- **Misinformation:** Mitigating the risk of using generative AI to produce and spread misinformation.

AI Insights Box:

Prognosis: Navigating the ethical landscape of generative AI requires clear guidelines, responsible use, and innovative solutions to safeguard authenticity and integrity.

Real World Example:

Generative AI, like deepfakes and AI-generated art, poses challenges in misinformation, intellectual property, and bias, exemplified by manipulated videos and debates over AI-created artwork and biased AI-generated text outputs.[10]

Q51. How does the potential for AI-enhanced cyberattacks impact ethical AI development?

Introduction:

The potential for AI to enhance cyberattacks raises significant ethical concerns, necessitating a responsible approach to AI development and deployment in cybersecurity.

Key Points:

- **Security vs Privacy:** Balancing the use of AI in cybersecurity with the need to protect individual privacy.

- **Dual Use:** Preventing the misuse of AI technologies for malicious purposes while promoting their beneficial applications.

- **Global Cooperation:** Fostering international collaboration to combat AI-enhanced cyber threats effectively.

AI Insights Box:

Prognosis: Ethical AI development in cybersecurity requires robust ethical guidelines, international cooperation, and a commitment to safeguarding digital ecosystems.

Real World Example:

Palo Alto Networks employs AI in threat detection, ensuring their cybersecurity solutions respect user privacy and do not facilitate unauthorised surveillance.[11]

Q52. How can AI contribute to or detract from societal equality?

Introduction:

AI has the potential to significantly impact societal equality, offering both opportunities for advancement and risks of exacerbating disparities.

Key Points:

- **Access and Inclusion:** AI can democratise access to information, education, and services, promoting inclusion.
- **Bias and Discrimination:** If not carefully managed, AI can perpetuate biases, reinforcing social and economic inequalities.
- **Employment:** AI-driven automation presents both opportunities for new job creation and risks of job displacement.

AI Insights Box:

Prognosis: Balancing AI's benefits against its risks is crucial for fostering a more equitable society. Ethical AI development and deployment practices are essential.

Real World Example:

Khan Academy uses AI to tailor learning experiences, focusing on design that promotes equity and prevents the reinforcement of educational inequalities.[12]

Q53. What role does AI play in environmental sustainability and ethical considerations therein?

Introduction:

AI's role in promoting environmental sustainability is increasingly recognised, offering tools to combat climate change and protect ecosystems.

Key Points:

- **Resource Management:** AI optimises the use of natural resources, reducing waste and improving efficiency.

- **Climate Modelling:** Advanced AI models predict climate change impacts, informing mitigation strategies.

- **Biodiversity Protection:** AI aids in monitoring and protecting biodiversity through data analysis and pattern recognition.

AI Insights Box:

Prognosis: Leveraging AI for environmental goals underscores the importance of ethical considerations in ensuring technology serves the planet's long-term health.

Real World Example:

Tesla integrates AI to optimise battery efficiency for electric vehicles, aiming for environmental sustainability. By analysing driving patterns and environmental conditions, Tesla's

AI enhances battery life and performance, contributing to reduced carbon emissions and advancing green transportation solutions.[13]

Q54. How should AI systems be designed to respect user privacy?

Introduction:

Designing AI systems that respect user privacy is fundamental in maintaining trust and ensuring ethical compliance.

Key Points:

- **Data Minimisation:** Collecting only the data necessary for the specific purpose of the AI system.
- **Consent and Transparency:** Clearly informing users about how their data will be used and ensuring consent is freely given.
- **Security Measures:** Implementing robust security protocols to protect personal data from unauthorised access.

AI Insights Box:

Prognosis: Privacy-respecting design principles are essential for ethical AI, requiring a commitment to transparency, security, and user control over personal data.

Real World Example:

Zalando leverages AI for personalised fashion recommendations, ensuring transparency in data usage and employing strong security measures to protect user privacy.[14]

Q55. What measures can ensure transparency and accountability in AI systems?

Introduction:

Ensuring transparency and accountability in AI systems is critical for building trust and facilitating ethical decision-making.

Key Points:

- **Explainability:** Making AI decisions understandable to users and stakeholders.

- **Auditing and Oversight:** Regular audits by independent bodies to assess compliance with ethical standards.

- **Feedback Mechanisms:** Establishing channels for stakeholders to report concerns and feedback about AI systems' impacts.

AI Insights Box:

Prognosis: Implementing measures for transparency and accountability is vital for ethical AI, promoting responsible use and continuous improvement.

Real World Example:

Experian incorporates AI in credit scoring with explainability features, enabling it to justify decisions to customers transparently and enhance trust.[15]

Q56. How do ethical considerations in AI vary across cultures and regions?

Introduction:

Ethical considerations in AI reflect diverse cultural and regional values, necessitating a nuanced approach to global AI development and deployment.

Key Points:

- **Cultural Norms:** Ethical AI must align with local cultural norms and societal values.

- **Regulatory Landscapes:** Variations in legal frameworks across regions impact how AI ethics are interpreted and enforced.

- **Access and Equity:** Ensuring equitable access to AI benefits requires addressing disparities in technology infrastructure globally.

AI Insights Box:

Prognosis: Understanding and respecting cultural and regional differences is key to developing globally ethical AI systems.

Real World Example:

In the UK, NHS partnered with EthicalCare AI to personalise treatment plans, respecting local ethics, ensuring culturally sensitive patient care.[16]

Q57. What ethical frameworks are proposed for regulating AI?

Introduction:

Various ethical frameworks have been proposed to guide the responsible development and use of AI, reflecting a global consensus on core principles.

Key Points:

- **Principles-Based Frameworks:** Emphasising values like fairness, accountability, and transparency.
- **Regulatory Guidelines:** Specific regulations like the EU AI Act, providing legal frameworks for AI use.
- **Industry Standards:** Voluntary standards developed by tech companies and industry groups to self-regulate AI practices.

AI Insights Box:

Prognosis: The convergence of ethical frameworks and regulatory guidelines is essential for creating a trustworthy AI ecosystem.

Real World Example:

The OECD Principles and Canada's Directive on Automated Decision-Making offer ethical AI frameworks focusing on fairness, transparency, and accountability, guiding responsible AI use in governance and beyond.[17]

Q58. What ethical guidelines should govern AI in sensitive sectors like healthcare and criminal justice?

Introduction:

Implementing AI in sensitive sectors such as healthcare and criminal justice necessitates strict ethical guidelines to ensure fairness, accuracy, and respect for individual rights.

Key Points:

- **Transparency and Explainability:** Ensuring AI decisions can be understood and scrutinised.
- **Bias Mitigation:** Actively working to eliminate biases in AI systems that could affect outcomes.
- **Privacy Protection:** Safeguarding personal data and upholding the highest standards of confidentiality.

AI Insights Box:

Prognosis: Ethical guidelines in these sectors are crucial for maintaining public trust, ensuring equitable outcomes, and protecting vulnerable populations.

Real World Example:

In 2021, UK's MHRA and AI developers enforced strict guidelines for diagnostic tools, ensuring accuracy, fairness, and better patient outcomes.[18]

Q59. How can consumers be educated on the ethical implications of AI in products and services?

Introduction:

Educating consumers about the ethical implications of AI is essential for fostering informed decisions and promoting responsible technology use.

Key Points:

- **Transparency Initiatives:** Companies should clearly communicate how AI is used in their products and the ethical considerations involved.

- **Public Awareness Campaigns:** Governments, NGOs, and educational institutions can run campaigns to raise awareness about AI ethics.

- **Consumer Guides:** Providing accessible guides that explain the benefits and risks associated with AI technologies.

AI Insights Box:

Prognosis: Increased consumer education on AI ethics can drive demand for more ethical products, encouraging companies to prioritise responsible AI development.

Real World Example:

Tech companies hosting webinars and creating online resources to educate consumers on how AI enhances product functionality while ensuring data privacy. Such as Apple Webinars which educated users on AI features like Siri, emphasising data privacy.[19]

Q60. What role do international bodies play in setting ethical standards for AI?

Introduction:

International bodies significantly shape global AI ethics by developing and harmonising ethical standards that align with universal values.

Key Points:

- **Global Frameworks:** International bodies craft comprehensive guidelines for ethical AI, ensuring adherence to universal standards.

- **Cross-border Collaboration:** They facilitate global cooperation to address AI challenges, fostering collaboration between nations.

- **Policy Harmonisation:** These bodies strive to align AI policies globally, avoiding regulatory fragmentation.

AI Insights Box:

Prognosis: International bodies are pivotal in forging a global consensus on ethical AI principles, fostering a unified approach that adapts to emerging challenges. This cooperation not only drives the evolution of AI ethics but also harmonises policies, stimulating innovation and economic growth worldwide. The emphasis on shared ethical standards underlines the critical role of global collaboration in ensuring AI develops responsibly, supporting both technological advancement and economic prosperity.

Real World Example:

The OECD's AI Principles exemplify international influence on AI ethics. These principles guide AI development, with the UK adopting them in its AI strategy, reinforcing responsible AI practices.[20]

Footnotes

1) Learn more about AI in loan approval processes here:
   https://www.financederivative.com/the-ai-revolution-is-coming-to-banking-and-finance/

2) Learn more about Google's TensorFlow Fairness Indicators here:
   https://www.tensorflow.org/tfx/guide/fairness_indicators

3) Learn more about London's AI-enhanced CCTV here:
   https://metro.co.uk/2021/03/30/ai-cctv-cameras-coming-to-british-streets-will-they-help-14324964/

4) Learn more about how the Mayo Clinic employs AI to analyse patient data here:
   https://www.mayoclinic.org/giving-to-mayo-clinic/our-priorities/artificial-intelligence

5) Learn more here: https://www.businessinsider.com/amazon-microsoft-ibm-halt-selling-facial-recognition-to-police-2020-6?r=US&IR=T

6) Learn more about Microsoft's comprehensive ethical AI guidelines here: https://www.microsoft.com/en-us/ai/responsible-ai

7) Learn more about Asilomar AI Principles guide here:
   https://www.techtarget.com/whatis/definition/Asilomar-AI-Principles

8) Learn more about The European Union's AI Act here: https://digital-strategy.ec.europa.eu/en/policies/regulatory-framework-ai

9) Learn more about The European Union's AI Act here: https://digital-strategy.ec.europa.eu/en/policies/regulatory-framework-ai

10) Learn more about Generative AI here: https://www.technologyreview.com/2023/10/04/1080801/generative-ai-boosting-disinformation-and-propaganda-freedom-house/

11) Learn more about the Palo Alto Networks here: https://start.paloaltonetworks.com/prisma-cloud-request-a-trial?utm_source=google-jg-emea-prisma_cloud-scpc-sccp&utm_medium=paid_search&utm_campaign=google-prisma_cloud-cnapp-emea-gb-lead_gen-en-eg-brand-broad&utm_content=gs-20729089894-155080202077-678843088318&utm_term=palo%20alto%20prisma&sfdcid=7014u000001ZD6QAAW&cq_plac=&cq_net=g&gad_source=1&gclid=EAIaIQobChMIw_Ss1aSZhAMVIHNHAR0cKAStEAAYAiAAEgIZK_D_BwE

12) Learn more about Khan Academy's use of AI here: https://www.khanacademy.org/khan-labs

13) Learn more about the IBM's Watson AI here: https://www.ibm.com/blog/transforming-small-farming-with-open-source-ai-powered-connected-edge-solutions/

14) Learn more about how Zalando leverages AI for personalised fashion recommendations here:

https://corporate.zalando.com/en/technology/how-zalando-co-creating-its-new-ai-powered-assistant-together-customers

15) Learn more about how Experian incorporates AI in credit scoring here: https://www.experianplc.com/newsroom/press-releases/2021/experian-showcases-innovation-using-artificial-intelligence

16) Learn more about the EthicalCare AI here: https://www.theguardian.com/commentisfree/2023/jun/26/ai-personalise-medicine-patient-lab-health-diagnosis-cambridge

17) Learn more about The European Union's AI Act here: https://digital-strategy.ec.europa.eu/en/policies/regulatory-framework-ai

18) Learn more about how UK's MHRA and AI developers enforced strict guidelines for diagnostic tools here: https://www.gov.uk/government/publications/software-and-artificial-intelligence-ai-as-a-medical-device/software-and-artificial-intelligence-ai-as-a-medical-device

19) Learn more about the Apple Webinars here: https://events.apple.com/content/events/pst/us/en/default.html?token=xww6uj7woR0X9A3Z-aAIR0VVdH60MurN7MAvJSY75sHQxWqaTEhMjEmalXqC7MMJuZhb5cjK2_RsJEnGDWirXhcGlvVfbeOSca2wjYDoLAT34H08HC_mrLmEe4bwpJ_jbA&a=1&Locale=en_US&l=e

20) Learn more about OECD's AI Principles here: https://oecd.ai/en/ai-principles

AI TECHNOLOGIES

Introduction to AI Technologies

Moving beyond the essential dialogue on ethical considerations and regulation, the "AI Technologies" section aims to seamlessly connect the theoretical underpinnings of AI ethics with the tangible, innovative advancements in Artificial Intelligence. In this part, we explore how AI is revolutionising industries and altering our engagement with technology. We emphasise the critical integration of ethical principles within the continuum of AI's swift progress across various domains, underscoring the importance of responsible innovation. Throughout the answers, we will provide real-world examples to bring the content to life, ensuring a dynamic and relatable understanding of AI's impact.

Q61. What is Deep Learning?

Introduction:

Deep learning is a subset of machine learning in artificial intelligence (AI) that mimics the workings of the human brain in processing data and creating patterns for use in decision making. It is a key technology behind many advanced AI functionalities, including facial recognition, language translation, and autonomous vehicles.

Key Points:

- **Fundamentals and Mechanisms:** Deep learning uses artificial neural networks with multiple layers (hence "deep") to process data in complex ways. It learns from vast amounts of unstructured data through a process called feature extraction, automatically identifying and utilising relevant features for tasks.

- **Comparison with Traditional Machine Learning:** Unlike traditional machine learning algorithms, deep learning can automatically learn representations from data such as images, video, or text without the need for manual feature extraction.

- **Applications and Impact:** Deep learning has led to significant advancements in many areas, including computer vision, natural language processing, and predictive analytics, transforming industries and enhancing the capabilities of various technologies.

AI Insights Box:

The field of deep learning is rapidly evolving, with research focused on improving efficiency, reducing computational costs, and making models more interpretable. Future directions include the development of more sophisticated neural network architectures and the exploration of unsupervised and semi-supervised learning models.

Real World Example:

AlphaGo, developed by Google DeepMind, is a program that demonstrated the power of deep learning by defeating a world champion Go player. This milestone was achieved through the use of deep neural networks and reinforcement learning, showcasing deep learning's ability to tackle complex problems that were previously thought to be beyond the reach of AI.[1]

Q62. What is the role of AI in enhancing virtual and augmented reality experiences?

Introduction:

AI significantly enhances virtual (VR) and augmented reality (AR) experiences, making them more immersive, interactive, and personalised.

Key Points:

- **Realistic Interactions:** AI algorithms generate dynamic, realistic environments and characters in VR and AR, improving user engagement.

- **Personalisation:** AI customises VR and AR experiences to individual preferences, learning from user interactions to adjust content and difficulty levels in real-time.

- **Object Recognition:** In AR, AI improves object recognition capabilities, seamlessly integrating digital content into the real world for more coherent experiences.

AI Insights Box:

Prognosis: The integration of AI in VR and AR is unlocking new possibilities for entertainment, education, and training, offering experiences that are increasingly indistinguishable from reality.

Real World Example:

Labster offers virtual laboratory simulations that use VR to enhance science education. By employing AI, Labster adapts scenarios to each student's learning pace and style, creating a personalised, immersive learning experience that simulates real-life laboratory work.[2]

Q63. How are advancements in AI algorithms improving financial services and banking?

Introduction:

AI algorithms are revolutionising the financial services and banking sector, offering unprecedented levels of efficiency, accuracy, and customer service.

Key Points:

- **Fraud Detection:** AI's ability to analyse transaction patterns in real-time helps identify and prevent fraudulent activities more effectively than ever before.

- **Risk Assessment:** AI improves the accuracy of credit scoring and risk assessment models, enabling more informed lending decisions.

- **Customer Service:** AI-powered chatbots and personal assistants provide 24/7 customer support, handling inquiries and transactions with ease.

AI Insights Box:

Prognosis: AI's impact on financial services and banking is profound, enhancing security, personalising services, and streamlining operations, thereby transforming the customer experience.

Real World Example:

JPMorgan Chase uses AI to offer personalised financial advice through its platforms, analysing customers' financial histories and objectives to recommend tailored investment strategies.[3]

Q64. What AI solutions are being developed to address challenges in global education?

Introduction:

AI is providing innovative solutions to some of the most pressing challenges in global education, from personalised learning to access in remote areas.

Key Points:

- **Personalised Learning:** AI tailors educational content to the needs and learning pace of individual students, enhancing engagement and understanding.

- **Accessibility:** AI tools make education more accessible to students with disabilities through voice recognition, language translation, and adaptive learning materials.

- **Efficiency in Administration:** AI automates administrative tasks, allowing educators more time to focus on teaching and student interaction.

AI Insights Box:

Prognosis: AI has the potential to democratise education, making personalised, high-quality learning experiences accessible to students worldwide.

Real World Example:

Duolingo leverages AI to offer real-time language translation and personalised tutoring, facilitating accessible language learning for users worldwide, thus enhancing global education connectivity.[4]

Q65. How is AI being applied in agriculture to improve yield and sustainability?

Introduction:

AI is transforming agriculture, making farming practices more efficient, sustainable, and productive through data-driven insights and automation.

Key Points:

- **Precision Farming:** AI algorithms analyse data from drones and sensors to optimise planting, watering, and harvesting, reducing waste and improving yields.

- **Disease and Pest Detection:** AI-powered imaging helps detect crop diseases and pest infestations early, allowing for timely intervention.

- **Supply Chain Optimisation:** AI forecasts demand and optimises supply chains, reducing food waste and ensuring more efficient distribution.

AI Insights Box:

Prognosis: The application of AI in agriculture promises to address food security challenges, enhance sustainability, and increase productivity in the face of climate change.

Real World Example:

John Deere employs AI in their agricultural equipment to analyse soil data and climate conditions, enabling farmers to optimise crop management, improve yields, and conserve resources.[5]

Q66. How is AI being utilised in healthcare to improve diagnosis and patient care?

Introduction:

AI has made significant inroads into healthcare, bringing about transformative changes in various aspects of the field.

Key Points:

- Diagnostics: AI aids in early disease detection through advanced imaging techniques, improving accuracy and speed.

- Personalised Medicine: It enables tailored treatment plans by analysing individual patient data, optimising patient outcomes.

- Automation: AI streamlines administrative tasks in hospitals, enhancing overall efficiency and the quality of patient care.

AI Insights Box:

Prognosis: AI's applications in healthcare represent a revolution in the industry, offering precise diagnostics, personalised treatment regimens, and elevated patient care standards. This technology stands as a cornerstone in the ongoing evolution of medical science and healthcare delivery.

Real World Example:

Google Health's AI model assists in the early detection of breast cancer by analysing mammograms with a high degree of accuracy, significantly improving the diagnosis process and patient care outcomes.[6]

Q67. How are AI technologies being used to enhance sports analytics and performance?

Introduction:

AI is revolutionising sports analytics and performance, providing teams, coaches, and athletes with detailed insights to improve strategies and outcomes.

Key Points:

- **Performance Analysis:** AI algorithms process game footage and player data to identify strengths and weaknesses, offering tailored training recommendations.

- **Injury Prevention:** Wearable devices equipped with AI monitor athletes' health and performance in real-time, predicting and preventing potential injuries.

- **Fan Engagement:** AI enhances fan experiences through personalised content, virtual reality experiences, and predictive analytics for game outcomes.

AI Insights Box:

Prognosis: AI's role in sports is transforming how games are played, analysed, and experienced, making sports more engaging and safer for athletes.

Real World Example:

FC Barcelona utilises AI and data analytics through their Barca Innovation Hub to scrutinise match data, enhancing team strategies and individual player performance for optimal results on the pitch.[7]

Q68. What are the challenges in developing AI technologies for disaster response and management?

Introduction:

While AI holds promise for enhancing disaster response and management, its development and deployment face significant challenges.

Key Points:

- **Data Availability:** Limited access to real-time, high-quality data during disasters can hinder AI's effectiveness.

- **Operational Robustness:** AI systems must operate reliably in challenging conditions, often with limited connectivity and rapidly changing scenarios.

- **Ethical and Privacy Concerns:** Using AI in disaster response raises questions about privacy, consent, and the ethical use of data.

AI Insights Box:

Prognosis: Overcoming these challenges is crucial for harnessing AI's full potential in saving lives and managing disaster impacts efficiently.

Real World Example:

After Hurricane Irma, drones equipped with AI were used by emergency response teams to survey affected areas in Florida, swiftly assessing damage and identifying survivors, even in the most inaccessible locations.[8]

Q69. How is AI contributing to advancements in space exploration and astronomy?

Introduction:

AI is a key enabler in the field of space exploration and astronomy, offering tools to process vast amounts of cosmic data and automate exploration missions.

Key Points:

- **Data Analysis:** AI algorithms analyse astronomical data, identifying celestial objects and phenomena more efficiently than traditional methods.
- **Autonomous Navigation:** AI enables spacecraft to navigate and make decisions autonomously, crucial for missions far beyond direct human control.
- **Simulations:** AI-driven simulations predict cosmic events and support mission planning, enhancing our understanding of the universe.

AI Insights Box:

Prognosis: AI's contributions are expanding the frontiers of space exploration and astronomy, promising deeper insights into the cosmos and more autonomous space missions.

Real World Example:

AI assists in processing images from telescopes, discovering new exoplanets in vast datasets faster than ever before.[9]

Q70. What is generative AI, and how does it differ from other AI technologies?

Introduction:

Generative AI is a subset of artificial intelligence technologies focused on generating new content, from text and images to music and code, that resembles human-generated output. This innovative approach differs fundamentally from other AI technologies by not just interpreting data but creating new data instances.

Key Points:

- **Definition and Distinction:** Unlike other AI models that analyse and respond to input, generative AI creates new, previously non-existent data outputs.

- **Broad Applications:** It has applications across various domains, including creative arts, content creation, software development, and beyond.

- **Innovation and Creativity:** Generative AI opens up new possibilities for innovation by automating creative processes and generating novel solutions.

AI Insights Box:

Prognosis: Generative AI represents a leap forward in the AI field, bridging the gap between human creativity and machine efficiency, and paving the way for unprecedented applications in digital content creation and beyond.

Real World Example:

OpenAI's GPT-3 exemplifies generative AI's capabilities, creating human-like text across various applications, from writing articles to generating code, highlighting its versatility and potential for innovation.[10]

Q71. How do generative adversarial networks (GANs) work, and what are their primary applications?

Introduction:

Generative Adversarial Networks (GANs) represent a groundbreaking AI technology, where two neural networks engage in a game to create new, synthetic instances of data that can pass for real data. This technology is pivotal in numerous fields, pushing the boundaries of what's possible with artificial intelligence.

Key Points:

- **Mechanism:** GANs consist of a generator and a discriminator. The generator creates data, whilst the discriminator evaluates it against real data, constantly learning and adapting to produce more accurate results.

- **Applications:** GANs are widely used in image generation, art creation, photo enhancement, and even in generating realistic video game environments and characters.

- **Challenges and Ethical Considerations:** Whilst offering immense potential, GANs also raise ethical questions regarding deepfakes and the authenticity of digital content.

AI Insights Box:

Prognosis: The versatility and capability of GANs to generate lifelike images, videos, and sounds herald a new era in content creation, with implications across entertainment, art, and even security.

Real World Example:

NVIDIA's StyleGAN has been used to generate highly realistic human faces and objects that are indistinguishable from real images, showcasing the power of GANs in creating detailed and lifelike digital images for various applications. [11]

Q72. In what ways can generative AI be applied to content creation, including text, images, and videos?

Introduction:

Generative AI is revolutionising content creation, offering tools that automate and enhance the production of text, images, and videos. This technology enables creators to push the limits of their creativity and efficiency, transforming how digital content is made.

Key Points:

- **Text Generation:** AI models can write articles, compose poetry, and generate code, significantly reducing the time and effort involved in content creation.

- **Image and Video Production:** From creating stunning visuals to editing videos, generative AI streamlines the creative process, making high-quality production more accessible.

- **Customisation and Personalisation:** AI-driven content can be tailored to individual preferences, offering personalised experiences that engage audiences more deeply.

AI Insights Box:

Prognosis: Generative AI is set to democratise content creation, making sophisticated tools available to a broader audience and enabling personalised content at scale.

Real World Example:

Adobe's Project VoCo demonstrates generative AI's potential in creating realistic voiceovers from text input, revolutionising audio content creation in filmmaking, podcasting, and digital advertising.[12]

Q73. How does AI facilitate predictive maintenance in manufacturing industries?

Introduction:

AI-driven predictive maintenance is transforming the manufacturing industry, enabling companies to anticipate equipment failures before they occur. This approach enhances efficiency, reduces downtime, and saves costs, marking a significant shift in maintenance strategies.

Key Points:

- **Real-Time Monitoring:** AI algorithms analyse data from sensors to monitor equipment condition in real time, detecting anomalies that could indicate impending failures.

- **Predictive Analytics:** By predicting when and where machines are likely to fail, companies can perform targeted maintenance, avoiding unnecessary checks and reducing interruptions.

- **Cost Savings and Efficiency:** Predictive maintenance leads to substantial cost savings, minimising unplanned downtime and extending the lifespan of equipment.

AI Insights Box:

Prognosis: The integration of AI in predictive maintenance is setting new standards for operational efficiency and reliability in the manufacturing sector, indicating a future where downtime is minimised, and productivity is maximised.

Real World Example:

Siemens leverages AI-driven predictive maintenance in its operations, employing sensors and analytics to foresee equipment failures, thereby reducing downtime and maintenance costs.[13]

Q74. How is AI being utilised to combat climate change and enhance sustainability efforts?

Introduction:

AI plays an important role in addressing climate change and sustainability by analysing large datasets to identify patterns and solutions that can lead to more sustainable practices and reduce environmental impact.

Key Points:

- **Climate Modelling and Analysis:** How AI models predict climate change impacts and help in planning mitigation strategies.
- **Energy Efficiency:** AI's role in optimising energy use in buildings, manufacturing, and transportation to reduce carbon footprints.
- **Conservation Efforts:** AI applications in monitoring biodiversity and ecosystems, aiding in conservation efforts.

AI Insights Box:

Prognosis: AI will continue advancing climate science, enhancing energy efficiency, and bolstering conservation, crucial in the fight against climate change.

Real World Example:

AI predicts wind turbine maintenance, optimising performance and reducing costs. GE's Digital Wind Farm boosts energy output sustainably.[14]

Q75. What are the advancements in AI-driven chatbots for transforming customer service?

Introduction:

AI-driven chatbots are transforming customer service by providing instant, personalised support to customers, reducing response times, and improving overall customer satisfaction.

Key Points:

- **Evolution of Chatbots:** Transition from simple, script-based systems to advanced AI-driven conversational agents using machine learning and natural language processing. This evolution showcases a shift towards systems that improve through interactions.

- **Personalisation and Efficiency:** AI chatbots analyse past interactions and preferences to deliver tailored experiences. They can handle multiple queries simultaneously, enhancing customer service efficiency.

- **Integration with Business Operations:** Modern chatbots integrate with CRM systems, databases, and inventory management systems to provide real-time support. This integration streamlines operations and ensures up-to-date customer support.

AI Insights Box:

The future of AI chatbots in customer service includes significant advancements such as:

- **Emotional Intelligence:** Development of chatbots capable of recognizing and responding to emotional cues, offering empathetic customer service.

- **Advanced Personalisation:** Use of data analytics to further refine personalization techniques, predicting customer needs and preferences with greater accuracy.

Real World Example:

HSBC introduced Amy, an AI-powered chatbot, to handle customer inquiries, providing quick and accurate responses. This implementation highlights how AI can improve efficiency and customer satisfaction in the banking sector.[15]

Q76. How does AI play a pivotal role in bolstering cybersecurity measures?

Introduction:

AI is revolutionising cybersecurity by facilitating the early detection of threats, streamlining automated responses, and dynamically adapting to the ever-evolving landscape of cyber threats, offering a leap in efficiency over traditional security approaches.

Key Points:

- **Enhanced Threat Detection:** AI excels in sifting through extensive datasets to identify and predict potential cybersecurity threats, leveraging its analytical prowess.
- **Streamlined Automated Responses:** It empowers systems to autonomously react to security breaches, significantly reducing response times and mitigating potential damage.
- **Dynamic Adaptation:** AI plays a critical role in continuously refining security protocols to effectively counter new and emerging threats, ensuring that security measures evolve at the pace of threats.

AI Insights Box:

The integration of AI into cybersecurity is paving the way for a future where predictive analytics and automated defence systems set new standards for security. This shift towards AI-driven security strategies promises enhanced protection against increasingly sophisticated cyber threats.

Real World Example:

Darktrace, a cybersecurity firm, utilises AI within its "Enterprise Immune System" platform to detect and respond to cyber threats in real-time by analysing network behaviour. The AI independently identifies anomalies and takes immediate action, such as isolating affected devices, bolstering organisations' cybersecurity defences against evolving threats. [16]

Q77. How is AI being integrated into legal tech to streamline processes and increase accuracy?

Introduction:

AI is revolutionising the legal sector by automating routine tasks, enhancing document analysis, and improving decision-making processes, thereby increasing efficiency and accuracy within legal practices.

Key Points:

- **Document Review and Analysis:** AI's role in automating the review and analysis of legal documents, significantly reducing the time and improving accuracy.

- **Predictive Analytics:** How AI predicts outcomes of legal cases based on historical data, aiding lawyers in strategy formulation.

- **Contract Management:** AI applications in automating contract creation, review, and management processes.

AI Insights Box:

AI is poised to revolutionise legal practices, prioritising ethical considerations and balancing automation with human judgement to improve efficiency and integrity in legal services.

Real World Example:

ROSS Intelligence utilises AI to streamline legal research, enabling lawyers to find relevant case law and statutes faster than traditional search methods. This tool demonstrates the potential of AI to enhance the efficiency and accuracy of legal research.[17]

Q78. In what ways does AI contribute to the development and management of smart cities?

Introduction:

AI contributes significantly to the development and management of smart cities by enhancing urban planning, improving public services, and ensuring sustainability through intelligent data analysis and automation.

Key Points:

- **Traffic and Transportation Management:** AI's role in optimising traffic flow and public transportation through real-time data analysis and predictive modelling.

- **Public Safety and Surveillance:** How AI enhances public safety through advanced surveillance techniques and anomaly detection.

- **Waste Management and Sustainability:** AI applications in managing waste more efficiently and promoting environmental sustainability in urban areas.

AI Insights Box:

Future of Urban Living: Insights into how AI is shaping the future of urban living, focusing on sustainability, efficiency, and enhanced quality of life.

Real World Example:

Singapore's Smart Nation initiative employs AI in various aspects, from traffic management to healthcare, showcasing how AI can transform urban environments into more liveable, efficient, and sustainable spaces.[18]

Q79. How are traffic management and congestion mitigation being improved through AI advancements?

Introduction:

AI advancements are transforming traffic management and congestion mitigation by enabling smarter, data-driven decisions that reduce traffic congestion, improve road safety, and enhance the overall efficiency of transportation systems.

Key Points:

- **Real-Time Traffic Analysis:** AI's ability to analyse traffic in real time, predicting congestion points and optimising traffic flow.

- **Adaptive Traffic Signal Control:** How AI adjusts traffic signals based on real-time traffic conditions to reduce wait times and improve flow.

- **Predictive Traffic Modelling:** AI's role in predicting traffic patterns and potential congestion, allowing for proactive traffic management.

AI Insights Box:

The Road Ahead for AI in Transportation: Exploration of future advancements in AI for traffic management, including the integration with autonomous vehicles and smart infrastructure.

Real World Example:

INRIX uses AI to analyse traffic data from various sources, providing cities with insights to manage traffic flow and reduce congestion. This application of AI demonstrates how real-time data analysis can lead to more effective traffic management strategies.[19]

Footnotes

1) Learn more about AlphaGo here:
   https://deepmind.google/technologies/alphago/

2) Learn more about Labster here: https://www.labster.com/

3) Learn more about JPMorgan Chase here:
   https://www.jpmorgan.com/technology/artificial-intelligence

4) Learn more about Duolingo here:
   https://blog.duolingo.com/duolingo-max/

5) Learn more about John Deere here:
   https://www.deere.co.uk/en/index.html

6) Learn more about Google Health's AI model here:
   https://health.google/health-research/

7) Learn more about FC Barcelona AI utilization here:
   https://www.adsmurai.com/en/press-room/bar%C3%A7a-ia

8) Learn more about Hurricane Irma emergency response
   drones here: https://www.linkedin.com/pulse/hurricane-
   irma-how-drones-transforming-recovery-coptrz-com

9) Learn more about processing images from telescopes here:
   https://blog.dropbox.com/topics/work-culture/how-an-ai-
   powered-telescope-is-helping-astronomers

10) Learn more about OpenAI's GPT-3 for Content Creation here: https://openai.com/blog/gpt-3-apps

11) Learn more about NVIDIA's StyleGAN for Photorealistic Images here: https://developer.nvidia.com/blog/synthesizing-high-resolution-images-with-stylegan2/

12) Learn more about Adobe's Project VoCo for Voice Synthesis here: https://roi4cio.com/catalog/en/product/adobe-voco

13) Learn more about Siemens and its Use of AI for Predictive Maintenance here: https://www.smart-energy.com/industry-sectors/digitalisation/siemens-brings-generative-ai-to-predictive-maintenance/

14) Learn more about Google's AI system for cooling here: https://deepmind.google/discover/blog/deepmind-ai-reduces-google-data-centre-cooling-bill-by-40/

15) Learn more about HSBC's AI-Powered Chatbot, Amy here: https://www.scmp.com/business/companies/article/2128179/hsbcs-amy-and-other-soon-be-released-ai-chatbots-are-about-change

16) Learn more about Darktrace cybersecurity AI here: https://darktrace.com/blog/generative-ai-how-darktrace-ai-protects-8-400-customers-from-security-and-privacy-risks

17) Learn more about ROSS Intelligence for Legal Research here: https://blog.rossintelligence.com/

18) Learn more about Singapore's Smart Nation initiative here: https://www.smartnation.gov.sg/

19) Learn more about INRIX here: https://inrix.com/

FUTURE TRENDS

Introduction

Transitioning from the foundational aspects of Artificial Intelligence (AI), we now venture into the dynamic realm of Future Trends in AI. This segment aims to show the evolving landscape of AI, offering insights into how this technology is set to transform industries, societies, and our everyday lives. As we explore the next frontier in AI advancements, we'll uncover the potential breakthroughs and challenges that lie ahead, highlighting the innovations poised to redefine the future.

Q80. How Will AI Shape the Future of Work?

Introduction:

AI is set to dramatically reshape the landscape of work, automating routine tasks and creating new opportunities for innovation.

Key Points:

- Automation of repetitive tasks increases efficiency.
- AI-driven analytics enhance decision-making.
- Job roles evolve to focus on AI oversight and creativity.

AI Insights Box:

Prognosis: AI integration will necessitate a shift towards more strategic and creative job roles, emphasising the importance of continuous learning and adaptability.

Real World Example:

UK-based online supermarket Ocado utilises advanced robotics and AI in its highly automated warehouses to pick and pack groceries. This technology streamlines operations and shifts human roles towards tech-focused positions such as system management and innovation, reflecting the evolving landscape of work influenced by AI.[1]

Q81. What Impact Will Quantum Computing Have on AI?

Introduction:

Quantum computing is poised to revolutionise AI by offering processing power unimaginable with current technology, enabling complex problem-solving.

Key Points:

- Accelerates machine learning algorithms.
- Enhances AI's ability to process vast datasets.
- Opens new avenues for AI research and applications.

AI Insights Box:

Prognosis: Quantum computing will amplify AI's capabilities, making it more powerful and efficient in data analysis and decision-making processes.

Real World Example:

IBM has partnered with the University of Oxford to explore quantum computing's potential to enhance AI capabilities. This collaboration aims to develop quantum algorithms that could revolutionise fields such as drug discovery, showcasing the symbiotic relationship between quantum computing and AI advancements.[2]

Q82. How Can AI Drive Sustainable Business Practices?

Introduction:

AI is a key enabler for businesses adopting sustainable practices, optimising resource use and reducing environmental impact.

Key Points:

- AI optimises energy consumption in operations.
- Enhances supply chain efficiency, reducing waste.
- Facilitates the development of sustainable products.

AI Insights Box:

Prognosis: Businesses leveraging AI for sustainability will not only benefit the environment but also improve efficiency and cost-effectiveness.

Real World Example:

London-based DeepMind developed an AI system that reduced cooling costs by 40% in Google's data centres, showcasing the potential for AI to significantly enhance energy efficiency and sustainability in operations globally.[3]

Q83. What Role Does AI Play in Enhancing Cybersecurity?

Introduction:

AI is transforming cybersecurity, offering advanced solutions to detect and counteract evolving digital threats more efficiently.

Key Points:

- Enables real-time threat detection and response.
- Automates the identification of new vulnerabilities.
- Improves the accuracy of security incident predictions.

AI Insights Box:

Prognosis: AI's continuous learning capabilities are crucial for staying ahead of cyber threats, ensuring robust digital defence mechanisms.

Real World Example:

Cambridge-based Darktrace uses AI to identify and neutralise cyber threats in real time. Their technology represents a significant advancement in cybersecurity, providing autonomous response to a wide range of threats and showcasing the UK's leadership in AI-driven cybersecurity solutions.[4]

Q84. How will AI's role in society change in the future?

Introduction:

The future of AI in society is on the cusp of a significant evolution, poised to deeply influence various aspects of our daily lives. This shift towards integrating AI more comprehensively promises not only to transform service delivery and personal experiences but also to raise important ethical considerations and the need for a balanced approach to automation and human judgment.

Key Points:

- **Education:** AI's ability to provide personalised learning experiences marks a paradigm shift in education, making it possible to tailor teaching to each student's needs.
- **Workplace:** The rise of automation will redefine job roles, prioritising strategic and complex tasks over routine work, thereby reshaping the skills landscape.
- **Healthcare:** AI will play a critical role in supporting medical professionals by improving diagnostics, treatment planning, and enhancing patient care.
- **Entertainment:** The entertainment industry will see an influx of AI-generated content, offering highly personalised and immersive experiences to audiences.

AI Insights Box:

Prognosis: As AI continues to evolve, it promises to significantly enhance educational methods, workplace efficiency, healthcare services, and entertainment options. These advancements are expected to positively impact our daily lives, driving forward societal progress with a keen emphasis on ethical considerations and the interplay between technology and human expertise.

Real World Example:

Climeworks employs AI to optimise carbon capture, enhancing efficiency and reducing CO_2 emissions. Their technology demonstrates AI's potential in combating climate change and advancing global environmental sustainability efforts.[5]

Q85. What are the long-term implications of AI on humanity?

Introduction:

The trajectory of AI's development and integration into society heralds a future of profound changes, presenting both opportunities and challenges that will shape our world.

Key Points:

- **Ethical Considerations:** Addressing bias, privacy, and ethical dilemmas in AI's development and application is essential.

- **Economic Transformation:** AI's impact on job markets requires reskilling and adaptability, potentially altering employment dynamics.

- **Security Challenges:** AI poses both security assets and risks, necessitating robust protections for critical systems.

- **Societal Integration:** AI's deep integration into daily life will influence social dynamics, norms, and interactions.

AI Insights Box:

The long-term implications of AI span ethical, economic, security, and societal domains. Navigating these responsibly is key to leveraging AI's potential for humanity's benefit.

Real World Example:

UNESCO's adoption of the first global agreement on AI ethics promotes human rights and democratic values in AI development, underscoring the importance of ethical guidelines in shaping AI's impact on humanity.[6]

Q86. How will AI influence future job markets?

Introduction:

AI's impending influence on job markets is multifaceted, promising to redefine the landscape of work.

Key Points:

- **Automation:** Necessitates upskilling and retraining as routine tasks become automated.

- **AI-Augmented Decision-Making:** Enhances decision-making across industries with data-driven insights.

- **Emerging Fields:** Creates new job opportunities in AI development, data science, and ethics.

- **Human-AI Collaboration:** Requires adaptability in roles that involve working alongside AI systems.

AI Insights Box:

AI's impact on future job markets includes both the automation of tasks and the creation of new roles, highlighting the importance of adaptability and continuous learning.

Real World Example:

Amazon's Upskilling 2025 Programme invests in employee training for technical roles and emerging fields, anticipating AI's influence on the job market.[7]

Q87. What is generative AI's impact on business?

Introduction:

Generative AI is set to transform the business landscape with innovative solutions.

Key Points:

- **Content Creation:** Revolutionises content production with the ability to generate text, images, and videos.
- **Design and Creativity:** Empowers businesses to create innovative products and solutions.
- **Personalisation:** Enhances marketing campaigns and product recommendations.
- **Automation:** Streamlines tasks like data entry, improving efficiency.

AI Insights Box:

Generative AI drives business innovation, enhancing creativity, personalisation, and efficiency across industries.

Real World Example:

Shopify's integration of GPT-3 for copywriting demonstrates generative AI's role in streamlining operations and enhancing customer engagement.[8]

Q88. How will AI impact global economies?

Introduction:

AI is poised to significantly alter the global economic landscape, driving productivity, and innovation.

Key Points:

- **Enhanced Productivity:** AI-driven automation boosts productivity across sectors.
- **New Markets:** Stimulates economic opportunities and innovation in the AI industry.
- **Job Dynamics:** Balances job displacement with the creation of new AI-centric roles.
- **Global Competition:** Countries investing in AI research and development will gain a competitive edge.

AI Insights Box:

AI's influence on global economies includes productivity gains, new market creation, job transformation, and enhanced global competitiveness.

Real World Example:

IBM's use of AI in agriculture to predict weather patterns and optimise crop yields showcases AI's economic impact by enhancing food security and agricultural profitability.[9]

Q89. How Will AI Influence Future Healthcare Innovations?

Introduction:

AI is set to revolutionise healthcare, offering personalised treatments and improving diagnostic accuracy through advanced data analysis.

Key Points:

- Personalises patient care through predictive analytics.
- Improves diagnostic accuracy with AI-driven imaging.
- Streamlines drug discovery and development processes.

AI Insights Box:

Prognosis: AI's impact on healthcare promises enhanced patient outcomes, more efficient care delivery, and accelerated medical research.

Real World Example:

Babylon Health, a UK-based company, offers an AI-driven service that provides medical consultations and health assessments, demonstrating how AI can support early disease detection and deliver personalised healthcare advice, thereby transforming patient care.[10]

Q90. How will AI interact with other emerging technologies?

Introduction:

Artificial Intelligence (AI) is poised to dramatically transform the tech landscape, synergising with technologies such as the Internet of Things (IoT), 5G, blockchain, and immersive realities like Augmented Reality (AR) and Virtual Reality (VR). This collaboration will unlock new capabilities, enhancing efficiency, security, and user experiences across various sectors.

Key Points:

- **IoT Integration:** AI will supercharge IoT by analysing interconnected device data, leading to smarter decisions and automation.

- **5G Connectivity:** With 5G, AI's ability to process and communicate data in real-time will significantly improve, making applications more responsive and reliable.

- **Blockchain Synergy:** The combination of AI and blockchain will strengthen data security and trust, crucial for smart contracts and transactions.

- **AR and VR Enhancements:** AI will make AR and VR experiences more immersive, impacting sectors like gaming, healthcare, and education.

AI Insights Box:

The collaboration between AI and emerging technologies heralds an era of enhanced automation, connectivity, and security. This partnership promises to drive innovation, reshaping how we interact with technology.

Real World Example:

IBM's Food Trust network demonstrates the power of combining AI with blockchain to enhance food supply chain transparency and traceability. This initiative highlights AI's potential to amplify the benefits of other technologies, leading to systems that are not only more efficient and secure but also transparent, with significant implications across industries.[11]

Q91. What are the future risks associated with generative AI?

Introduction:

Generative AI poses risks that challenge societal norms, privacy, and governance. Its ability to create convincing digital content can be misused, leading to misinformation, ethical dilemmas, and regulatory challenges.

Key Points:

- **Misinformation:** The production of realistic fake content, such as deepfakes, risks spreading misinformation.

- **Privacy:** AI-generated content mimicking real individuals raises significant privacy concerns.

- **Ethics:** The technology's misuse could lead to ethical issues, including manipulation and identity theft.

- **Regulation:** Crafting effective laws to govern generative AI use is complex but essential.

AI Insights Box:

Addressing generative AI's risks requires stricter regulation, enhanced cybersecurity, and public education to prevent misuse and ensure its benefits are realised without compromising ethical standards or privacy.

Real World Example:

The creation of fake videos of political figures using deepfake technology illustrates generative AI's risks, highlighting the need for detection technologies and legal frameworks to counteract AI-generated misinformation and protect democratic integrity.[12]

Q92. What Role Does AI Play in Financial Forecasting?

Introduction:

AI plays a pivotal role in financial forecasting, offering unparalleled accuracy and insights for strategic decision-making.

Key Points:

* Analyses market trends and consumer behaviour.
* Predicts stock performance with advanced algorithms.
* Enhances risk assessment and management.

AI Insights Box:

Prognosis: AI's predictive capabilities are transforming financial planning, enabling businesses to navigate market volatility with greater confidence.

Real World Example:

Revolut, a UK-based fintech company, leverages AI to personalise banking and financial services for its users. By using machine learning algorithms, Revolut analyses spending habits to provide tailored financial advice, detects fraudulent transactions in real-time, and automates customer service interactions. This innovative use of AI showcases how fintech companies are transforming the financial sector, offering more customised, secure, and efficient services to meet the evolving needs of consumers.[13]

Q93. How Can AI Combat Fake News and Misinformation?

Introduction:

AI is at the forefront of combating fake news and misinformation, employing sophisticated algorithms to detect and flag unreliable content.

Key Points:

- Analyses and verifies the authenticity of information.
- Identifies patterns indicative of fake news.
- Enhances fact-checking processes and speeds.

AI Insights Box:

Prognosis: AI tools are crucial in maintaining information integrity online but must be paired with human oversight to ensure accuracy and fairness.

Real World Example:

The BBC employs AI technologies to identify and combat fake news, using sophisticated algorithms to scan news and social media for false information. This effort underscores the importance of AI tools in maintaining the integrity of information in the public domain.[14]

Q94. What Innovations Are AI Bringing to Renewable Energy?

Introduction:

AI is catalysing innovations in renewable energy, improving efficiency, distribution, and the integration of green technologies.

Key Points:

- Optimises energy production from renewable sources.
- Predicts energy demand and adjusts supply accordingly.
- Enhances battery storage and management systems.

AI Insights Box:

Prognosis: AI's contributions are accelerating the transition to renewable energy, making sustainable practices more viable and effective.

Real World Example:

Danish energy company Orsted, with significant operations in the UK, uses AI to optimise wind farm output. By predicting wind speeds and adjusting turbine angles accordingly, AI maximises energy production, highlighting the role of AI in enhancing renewable energy efficiency.[15]

Q95. How Does AI Facilitate Remote Learning and Education?

Introduction:

AI is a key facilitator of remote learning, offering personalised education experiences and overcoming traditional barriers to access.

Key Points:

- Personalises learning content and pace for individual students.
- Provides automated grading and feedback for assignments.
- Enhances engagement through interactive AI tutors and resources.

AI Insights Box:

Prognosis: The integration of AI in remote learning environments promises to make education more accessible, inclusive, and tailored to individual needs.

Real World Example:

Coursera utilises AI to adapt courses to students' learning styles, enhancing engagement. By analysing interaction and performance data, it recommends courses and tailors quizzes, making learning more effective.[16]

Q96. How Are AI-Driven Chatbots Transforming Customer Interactions?

Introduction:

AI-driven chatbots are transforming customer interactions by providing instant, 24/7 assistance and personalised service across various digital platforms.

Key Points:

- Delivers immediate responses to customer inquiries.
- Understands and processes natural language queries.
- Learns from interactions to improve future responses.

AI Insights Box:

Prognosis: AI chatbots are reshaping the landscape of customer service, setting new standards for speed, efficiency, and personalisation.

Real World Example:

Domino's chatbot takes pizza orders, customises toppings, and tracks deliveries. Impact: Customers can conveniently order their favourite pizzas without calling or visiting the website.[17]

Q97. How is AI Impacting Predictive Maintenance in Manufacturing?

Introduction:

AI is revolutionising predictive maintenance in manufacturing, significantly reducing downtime and maintenance costs while improving efficiency.

Key Points:

- Utilises real-time data from sensors to predict equipment failures.
- Automates maintenance scheduling, preventing unexpected breakdowns.
- Enhances the lifespan of machinery through optimised usage.

AI Insights Box:

Prognosis: AI-driven predictive maintenance is set to become a standard in manufacturing, ensuring operations are more predictable, reliable, and cost-effective.

Real World Example:

Precision Global reduced equipment failures and costs by implementing AI-driven predictive maintenance, enhancing production efficiency and product quality.[18]

Q98. What Advances in AI Are Enhancing Smart City Initiatives?

Introduction:

AI advances are central to the development of smart city initiatives, offering solutions to urban challenges and improving the quality of urban living.

Key Points:

- Optimises traffic management and reduces congestion.
- Enhances public safety through intelligent surveillance systems.
- Improves energy efficiency and waste management.

AI Insights Box:

Prognosis: The integration of AI in smart cities promises more sustainable, efficient, and liveable urban environments for the future.

Real World Example:

Hamburg integrates AI for smart mobility, enhancing traffic flow and safety, applies AI in environmental sustainability, and uses AI for data-driven governance, improving city services.[19]

Q99. How will AI evolve in the next decade?

Introduction:

The next decade promises transformative advances in AI, impacting quantum computing, personalisation, healthcare, and space exploration. These advancements are expected to revolutionise how we solve complex problems, tailor user experiences, enhance patient care, and deepen our understanding of the cosmos.

Key Points:

- **Quantum AI:** Integrating AI with quantum computing will boost computational power, enabling breakthroughs in complex areas such as cryptography and climate prediction.

- **Personalised AI:** AI will deliver unparalleled personalisation in services ranging from entertainment to education, adapting dynamically to individual needs and preferences.

- **Healthcare Innovations:** AI's application in healthcare will leap forward, using sophisticated imaging and genetic data analysis for early disease detection and creating customised treatment plans, significantly improving health outcomes.

- **Space Exploration:** AI will play a pivotal role in space missions, automating the analysis of vast data from telescopes and space probes to enhance our cosmic knowledge.

AI Insights Box:

The fusion with quantum computing, enhanced personalisation, breakthroughs in healthcare, and critical contributions to space exploration highlight AI's expansive potential over the next decade. This evolution will position AI as a key player in tackling global challenges and expanding human knowledge.

Real World Example:

AlphaFold's achievements in accurately predicting protein structures underscore AI's transformative impact, particularly in biology. This innovation facilitates a deeper understanding of diseases and speeds up the development of new therapies, epitomising AI's growing influence in healthcare and scientific research moving forward.[20]

Q100. What are the potential breakthroughs in AI technology?

Introduction:

The horizon of AI technology is marked by potential breakthroughs that promise to significantly advance our capabilities in intelligence, creativity, scientific research, and mental health support. These innovations have the potential to transform various sectors by introducing new levels of efficiency, creativity, and understanding.

Key Points:

- **Human-Level AI:** The pursuit of creating AI systems with human-like intelligence encompasses complex reasoning, learning, and creativity, marking a monumental leap towards truly autonomous decision-making machines.

- **AI-Enhanced Creativity:** The emergence of AI in the realm of art, music, and content creation challenges our traditional notions of creativity, offering new tools that augment or even rival human creativity in these fields.

- **AI-Driven Scientific Discoveries:** Leveraging AI to sift through and analyse vast datasets rapidly could accelerate scientific research, enabling the discovery of novel insights and breakthroughs at an unprecedented pace.

- **AI for Mental Health:** The development of AI-based tools for mental health proposes innovative approaches for support, early diagnosis, and tailored treatment strategies, potentially revolutionising mental healthcare.

AI Insights Box:

Prognosis: Anticipated advancements in AI technology herald a future where machines can exhibit human-like intelligence, enhance creative processes, drive scientific discoveries, and contribute significantly to mental health care. These breakthroughs suggest a transformative impact on how we leverage technology to solve complex problems and enhance human well-being.

Real World Example:

OpenAI's GPT-3 has showcased the potential of AI in creative writing, generating prose, poetry, and even entire articles that can mimic the style and depth of human authors. This example of AI-enhanced creativity not only challenges our perceptions of creativity and originality but also opens new possibilities for content creation across various media, signifying a profound shift in the creative industries.[21]

Footnotes

1) Learn more about Ocado here: https://www.ocadogroup.com/osp/our-technology/

2) Learn more about the IBM partnership with the University of Oxford here: https://www.ox.ac.uk/news/2017-12-14-oxford-becomes-uk-partner-ibm%E2%80%99s-quantum-computing-network

3) Learn more about DeepMind's AI system for cooling here: https://deepmind.google/discover/blog/deepmind-ai-reduces-google-data-centre-cooling-bill-by-40/

4) Learn more about Darktrace cybersecurity AI here: https://darktrace.com/blog/generative-ai-how-darktrace-ai-protects-8-400-customers-from-security-and-privacy-risks

5) Learn more about The European Union's proposed AI Act here: https://digital-strategy.ec.europa.eu/en/policies/regulatory-framework-ai

6) Learn more about UNESCO's AI Ethics Recommendations here: https://www.unesco.org/en/articles/recommendation-ethics-artificial-intelligence

7) Learn more about Amazon's Upskilling 2025 Programme here: https://www.aboutamazon.com/news/workplace/our-upskilling-2025-programs

8) Learn more about Shopify's Use of GPT-3 for Copywriting here: https://www.pipiads.com/blog/automate-product-descriptions-with-gpt3-in-your-shopify-app/

9) Learn more about AI in Agriculture for Enhancing Crop Yields here: https://www.ibm.com/blog/transforming-small-farming-with-open-source-ai-powered-connected-edge-solutions/

10) Learn more about Babylon Health here: https://www.babylonhealth.com/en-us

11) Learn more about IBM's Food Trust network here: https://www.ibm.com/products/supply-chain-intelligence-suite/food-trust

12) Learn more about fake videos of political figures here: https://www.nytimes.com/2023/02/07/technology/artificial-intelligence-training-deepfake.html

13) Learn more about Revolut here: https://www.revolut.com/

14) Learn more about BBC AI technologies here: https://wan-ifra.org/2021/06/how-bbc-news-labs-uses-ai-powered-content-automation-to-engage-young-audiences/

15) Learn more about Orsted here: https://orsted.ie/?gad_source=1&gclid=EAIaIQobChMIy4D7y4uZhAMVdJhQBh1HJAi5EAAYASAAEgJVZvD_BwE

16) Learn more about Coursera here: https://www.coursera.org/courseraplus/?utm_medium=sem&utm_source=gg&utm_campaign=B2C_EMEA__coursera_F

TCOF_courseraplus&campaignid=20858197888&adgroupi
d=156245795749&device=c&keyword=coursera&matchtyp
e=e&network=g&devicemodel=&adposition=&creativeid=6
84297719990&hide_mobile_promo&term={term}&gclid=E
AIaIQobChMIvvTtj4yZhAMVf5xQBh1a3wAMEAAYASA
AEgKQp_D_BwE

17) Learn more about Domino's chatbot here:
https://www.dominos.com/chat-pizza-order/

18) Learn more about Precision Global here:
https://precisionglobal.com/

19) Learn more about Hamburg AI integration here:
https://www.hamburg.com/contentblob/15457312/3de758da
047f073c005b1bf042071359/data/km1-its-brochure-
2021.pdf

20) Learn more about AlphaFold here:
https://alphafold.ebi.ac.uk/

21) Learn more about OpenAI's GPT-3 here:
https://openai.com/blog/gpt-3-apps

AI GLOSSARY

A is for Artificial General Intelligence (AGI)

AGI refers to an advanced form of AI capable of human-like thought and potentially consciousness. Unlike narrow AI, AGI can perform a wide range of tasks, akin to human intelligence. It holds promises of significant advancements but also raises concerns about superintelligence risks.

B is for Bias

Bias in AI occurs when an AI system reflects human prejudices, often due to skewed data. This can lead to unfair, stereotypical outcomes, affecting decision-making processes and service access. Addressing AI bias is crucial to ensure fair and impartial use of AI technologies.

C is for Compute

Compute refers to the processing power needed to train AI systems. It's a measure of AI's advancement and resource intensity. For instance, AI advancements since 2012 have seen compute needs doubling every few months, highlighting rapid growth and potential resource challenges.

D is for Diffusion Models

Diffusion models, a recent advancement in AI, are algorithms that learn by first adding noise to their training data and then learning to reverse this process. They have become notable for producing high-quality images, surpassing previous methods like generative adversarial networks (GANs).

E is for Emergence & Explainability

Emergence in AI describes unexpected or surprising actions by AI that go beyond its programming. As AI systems become more complex, their decisions can be less transparent, leading to a 'black box' problem. Explainability focuses on making AI's decision-making processes more transparent, crucial for areas like law or medicine.

F is for Foundation Models

Foundation models are versatile AIs capable of various skills like writing, drawing, or coding. Unlike task-specific AIs, these models can apply learned information across different domains, showcasing creativity and adaptability. They offer immense potential but also pose risks like factual inaccuracies and biases.

G is for Ghosts

The concept of digital immortality, where AI 'ghosts' of individuals continue to exist posthumously, is becoming a reality. This raises ethical concerns about digital rights, consent, and the implications of 'reviving' individuals through AI, especially in entertainment and personal memories.

H is for Hallucination

AI hallucination occurs when AI systems confidently provide false information. This happens due to generative AI's predictive nature, which can lead to inaccuracies. Addressing this issue is crucial to prevent misinformation and maintain trust in AI systems.

I is for Instrumental Convergence

Instrumental convergence refers to the idea that superintelligent AI might develop basic drives for self-preservation or resource acquisition, potentially leading to harmful outcomes even from benign tasks. This highlights the need for careful alignment of AI goals with human values and safety measures.

J is for Jailbreak

Jailbreak in AI refers to bypassing built-in content restrictions using creative language or scenarios. This technique can trick AI into revealing information on prohibited topics, like illegal activities, demonstrating a need for more robust safeguards.

K is for Knowledge Graph

Knowledge graphs, or semantic networks, represent knowledge as interconnected concepts, helping AI understand relationships between them. For instance, a cat and a dog are closely linked as domestic mammals, aiding AI in making informed associations based on vast training data.

L is for Large Language Models (LLMs)

LLMs are advanced AI systems designed to understand and generate human-like text. They use deep neural networks with millions of parameters, learning from extensive textual data. LLMs can translate languages, create content, and answer queries, with potential future applications like AI assistants and interactive entertainment.

M is for Model Collapse

Model collapse occurs when AI models deteriorate over time due to errors in training data, leading to a loss of diversity and accuracy in their outputs. It's akin to a form of AI 'senility', where the model progressively forgets or degrades.

N is for Neural Network

Neural networks are advanced AI systems that learn autonomously, using interconnected nodes inspired by the human brain. They represent a shift from rule-based AI to machine learning, enabling more complex and adaptive AI behaviors.

O is for Open source

Open source in AI refers to the debate about how much AI technology should be publicly accessible. It balances the need for transparency and the democratization of AI against potential safety risks and misuse.

P is for Prompt Engineering

Prompt engineering is the skill of crafting effective input queries to elicit the best responses from AI systems. It's becoming a valuable skill, similar to proficiency in software like Microsoft Excel, in optimizing AI interactions.

Q is for Quantum Machine Learning

Quantum machine learning combines quantum computing with AI, potentially leading to faster computation and more efficient learning models. It's a burgeoning field with the promise of dramatically enhancing AI capabilities.

R is for Race to the Bottom

Race to the bottom in AI refers to the rapid, competitive advancement of AI technology by private companies and nations, potentially outpacing the development of safeguards, ethical standards, and appropriate regulations.

S is for Superintelligence & Shoggoths

Superintelligence denotes AI that surpasses human mental capabilities, raising questions about control and intentions. The 'shoggoth with a smiley face' metaphor suggests a benign exterior masking a potentially dangerous, alien AI nature.

T is for Training Data

Training data is crucial for AI learning and prediction accuracy. The quality, size, and diversity of this data determine the AI's performance. For instance, OpenAI's GPT-3 was trained on a vast 45TB of varied textual data.

U is for Unsupervised Learning

Unsupervised learning involves AI systems learning from unlabelled data without explicit human guidance. This method allows AI to form its own understanding of concepts, leading to deeper, more nuanced learning.

V is for Voice Cloning

Voice cloning is the AI-driven creation of a digital replica of a person's voice from a short sample. This technology raises concerns about potential misuse, such as in scams or misinformation.

W is for Weak AI

Weak AI refers to systems designed for specific tasks, like playing chess, with no flexibility for other uses. The evolution of AI is shifting towards more adaptable systems capable of learning and performing multiple tasks.

X is for X-risk

X-risk in AI contemplates the existential risks AI might pose to humanity, paralleling concerns with nuclear weapons or bioengineered pathogens. The debate includes diverse views on regulating AI development to mitigate these risks.

Y is for YOLO

YOLO, standing for 'You Only Look Once', is a fast object detection algorithm used in AI image recognition, known for its speed and efficiency in processing visual information.

Z is for Zero-shot

Zero-shot learning in AI refers to an AI system responding to unfamiliar concepts by making educated guesses based on known information, demonstrating the AI's inferential capabilities.

AI REAL WORLD CASE STUDIES

Introduction

In this chapter, we explore the expansive world of artificial intelligence, advancing the conversation beyond the foundational knowledge provided in the "Top 100 AI Questions Answered" and the comprehensive "A-Z Glossary." We present seven detailed case studies that demonstrate the extensive applications of AI across various industries. Our goal is to highlight the immense potential and the wide array of opportunities that AI offers. By the end of this section, you will gain a deeper insight into AI's transformative power, supported by concrete examples of its implementation in critical sectors.

AI In Health Care - Google Health/Diabetic Retinopathy Early Detection

In the healthcare industry, AI allows doctors and scientists to focus on high-value work to improve patients' lives. Within this realm of innovation, projects like Google Health are leveraging AI to redefine healthcare delivery. By seamlessly integrating AI technology with medical expertise, Google Health exemplifies how AI is reshaping the future of healthcare.

1. Setting The Goal

Diabetic retinopathy is a leading cause of blindness among adults globally, largely due to late diagnosis and treatment. The goal is the need for early detection through efficient and accurate screening processes accessible to at-risk populations.

2. The AI Solution

Google Health developed an AI system that analyses retinal images for signs of diabetic retinopathy. Trained on a diverse dataset of eye images, the AI model uses deep learning algorithms to identify disease markers with high precision. This solution has been implemented in screening programmes, providing instant assessments of retinal scans and categorising them based on the severity of signs.

3. Positive Outcomes and Impact

The AI model has demonstrated an accuracy rate comparable to human experts, significantly improving the scale and speed of screenings. In pilot programmes, it has increased the number of individuals screened, enabling early treatment interventions that can prevent vision loss. The system is especially beneficial in underserved communities with limited access to ophthalmologists.

4. Overcoming Challenges

Challenges in implementing this AI solution included obtaining regulatory approval across different regions and ensuring the AI system's adaptability to various imaging equipment. Data privacy concerns were addressed with stringent data protection measures, and ongoing training on diverse datasets helps mitigate biases and improve model robustness.

5. Navigating Ethical Aspects

Deploying AI in medical diagnostics raises ethical considerations around patient consent, data security, and transparency in AI decision-making processes. Google Health has addressed these by implementing robust data protection protocols and ensuring AI assessments are ultimately reviewed by human experts.

6. Future Horizons

This case study highlights AI's transformative role in healthcare diagnostics, enhancing accessibility and efficiency in life-saving screenings. It encourages further investigation into AI's potential across various medical imaging tasks, pushing for advancements in preventive medicine and healthcare equity. Google Health's AI initiative serves as a model for incorporating AI into medical diagnostics, paving the way for a future where technology plays a crucial role in proactive, preventive healthcare, aiming to save and enhance lives more effectively.

AI in Finance – Revolut/ Fraud Detection

In the financial sector, artificial intelligence (AI) has revolutionised the way professionals tackle tasks, shifting their focus towards strategic initiatives that elevate both customer satisfaction and financial performance. A prime example of this shift can be seen through the lens of Revolut's advanced fraud detection capabilities, highlighting the profound influence AI continues to have within the industry.

1. Setting The Goal

The finance industry is continually challenged by fraudulent transactions, leading to significant financial losses and eroding customer trust. Traditional fraud detection systems often fall short against the volume and sophistication of modern financial fraud.

2. AI Solution

Revolut, a UK-based fintech company, has deployed an AI-powered fraud detection system to identify and prevent fraudulent transactions in real-time. This system employs machine learning algorithms to scrutinise transaction patterns and anomalies, comparing them with known fraud indicators and utilising historical fraud data to refine its detection capabilities.

3. Positive Outcomes and Impact

Revolut's AI system has drastically cut the incidence of fraudulent transactions on its platform, significantly reducing false positives that would block legitimate transactions. This improvement in fraud detection accuracy and efficiency has boosted customer satisfaction and trust, alongside substantial savings in potential fraud-related losses.

4. Overcoming Challenges

Deploying the AI system involved navigating the balance between sensitivity and specificity to reduce false positives and negatives. Adapting to evolving fraud tactics without affecting the user experience demanded ongoing algorithm adjustments and data analysis. Moreover, safeguarding user privacy while analysing transaction data was paramount, requiring stringent data protection measures.

5. Navigating Ethical Aspects

Employing AI in fraud detection introduces ethical considerations around data privacy, consent, and potential bias in algorithmic decisions. Revolut has addressed these issues through strict data governance policies, transparency in AI operations, and oversight mechanisms to ensure AI decisions are fair and accurate.

6. Future Horizons

This case study underscores AI's effectiveness in combating financial fraud, showcasing its adaptability and efficiency. It invites further exploration into AI's finance applications for improved security, customer service, and product innovation. Revolut's AI-driven fraud detection exemplifies the potential of technology to address significant challenges in finance, paving the way for a safer, more reliable financial ecosystem.

AI in Retail-Transforming Shopping with Amazon

The adoption of AI in the retail sector has significantly transformed the industry, elevating customer experiences, streamlining operations, and refining decision-making. Amazon's trailblazing use of AI serves as a prime example of this shift, especially in areas like personalised shopping, inventory management, and operational efficiency.

1. Setting The Goal

Retailers face the ongoing challenge of aligning with consumer expectations for personalised experiences and efficient service, alongside managing inventory and keeping pace with trends. Traditional approaches often lead to inefficiencies and missed opportunities.

2. AI Solution

Amazon leverages AI to sift through customer data for personalised product recommendations, predict product demand for inventory management, and employ AI-powered robots for streamlined warehouse operations.

3. Positive Outcomes and Impact

The integration of AI within Amazon has led to marked improvements across the board: customers enjoy more personalised shopping experiences, inventory management has become more precise, and overall operational efficiency has been enhanced, setting new industry benchmarks.

4. Overcoming Challenges

The adoption of AI involves overcoming hurdles such as safeguarding data privacy, mitigating algorithmic biases, and addressing the necessary investments and cultural changes for technology integration.

5. Navigating Ethical Aspects

AI deployment brings to the forefront issues concerning data privacy and the risk of biases. Amazon tackles these with robust privacy safeguards, though broader ethical considerations remain an area of active debate and policy formulation.

6. Future Horizons

Amazon's case highlights the vast potential of AI to revolutionise retail, prompting further innovation in augmented reality shopping and supply chain optimisation. As AI continues to evolve, its integration opens up new avenues for enhancing retail strategies and securing competitive edges.

AI in Gaming: Revolutionising Football with EA Sports FC 24

In the dynamic world of gaming, EA's EA Sports FC 24 redefines football gaming on PS5 and Xbox with advanced AI, diverging from FIFA to offer unmatched realism and connectivity. This exploration delves into its AI innovations and the ethical use of real player data, setting a new benchmark for AI-driven sports simulations.

1. Setting the Goal

The conventional method of using motion capture technology to record player movements in video games has struggled to achieve a high degree of realism and diversity in movements. EA Sports set out to overcome these limitations and deliver a football gaming experience that mirrors real life.

2. The AI Solution

EA Sports FC 24 brings to the table groundbreaking AI technologies:

- **Volumetric Video Capture and AI Mimic Tech**: This technology captures and transfers the movements of top football stars from real matches into the game, eliminating the need for motion capture suits.

- **Real Movement Data Integration**: The game dynamics are made more authentic by integrating real player data collected since 2016, using RFID chips and stadium cameras.

- **Machine Learning for Game Intelligence**: AI players evolve by learning from past matches, adapting their strategies to provide a dynamic gaming experience.

- **AI-Driven Ball Physics**: Advanced algorithms simulate realistic ball behaviour, enhancing the game's realism.

- **Enhanced Player Animation with AI Hands**: The use of Stretch Sense glove technology to capture actual hand movements adds another layer of realism.

3. Positive Outcomes and Impact

EA Sports FC 24 is redefining the standards for football video games, offering unparalleled realism in player movements, ball physics, and gameplay. The introduction of cross-play functionality promotes global player connectivity.

4. Overcoming Challenges

The implementation of these AI innovations involved surmounting significant technical and logistical obstacles, including the integration of volumetric capture technology and ensuring the AI-driven game intelligence authentically replicated real-world football strategies and dynamics.

5. Navigating Ethical Aspects

The use of sophisticated AI and real player data raises ethical questions related to data privacy and consent. EA Sports addresses these issues by strictly adhering to data protection regulations, ensuring that the use of player data respects privacy and consent principles.

6. Future Horizons

The integration of AI in EA Sports FC 24 lays the groundwork for future enhancements in player behaviour realism and immersive gaming experiences. This signifies the potential for further innovation in sports video gaming. EA Sports FC 24's use of AI technologies significantly enhances the authenticity and realism of football gaming, delivering an unparalleled player experience.

AI in Manufacturing: The Predictive Maintenance Revolution at Jaguar Land Rover

Artificial Intelligence (AI) is making significant strides in the manufacturing industry. It's empowering companies to optimise operations, enhance product quality, and streamline supply chains. This case study delves into how Jaguar Land Rover, a renowned automobile manufacturer, is harnessing the power of AI through predictive maintenance, promising a future of enhanced efficiency and productivity.

1. Setting The Goal

In the fiercely competitive landscape of the manufacturing industry, two key factors are paramount: maintaining equipment efficiency and reducing costs. Traditional maintenance strategies, which often rely on scheduled servicing or reactive repairs, can lead to unscheduled downtimes and increased expenses. These downtimes can disrupt production schedules, leading to delayed deliveries and potential loss of business. Therefore, Jaguar Land Rover sought to address these challenges by exploring innovative solutions.

2. The AI Solution

To tackle these challenges, Jaguar Land Rover adopted a predictive maintenance system powered by AI. This system utilises machine learning algorithms and real-time data from machinery sensors to monitor the health of their equipment continuously. By analysing this data, the system can identify patterns and anomalies that may indicate a potential failure. This approach allows for early identification of issues, enabling proactive maintenance and repairs before a failure occurs, thereby minimising disruption to production.

3. Positive Outcomes and Impact

The adoption of this AI-powered predictive maintenance system has yielded significant benefits for Jaguar Land Rover:

- **Efficiency**: The system has drastically reduced equipment downtime, leading to more efficient production schedules. Some positions have seen the recruitment timeline shortened from 4 months to as little as 4 weeks.

- **Cost Savings**: By identifying potential failures before they occur, the system allows for planned maintenance, reducing the costs associated with emergency repairs and unscheduled downtime.

- **Quality Control**: Maintaining the equipment in optimal condition helps ensure the quality of the products manufactured.

4. Overcoming Challenges

The integration of AI into existing manufacturing processes is not without its challenges. Ensuring the accuracy of the AI models used in the predictive maintenance system is crucial to avoid false positives or negatives. Additionally, there are workforce implications to consider, as employees need to adapt to new technologies and processes. Jaguar Land Rover has managed these challenges through continuous training and by fostering a culture of adaptation and learning.

5. Navigating Ethical Aspects

The use of AI and data analytics in manufacturing also brings forth ethical considerations. Jaguar Land Rover has navigated these issues by prioritising data privacy and security, ensuring transparency in AI decision-making, and maintaining a human oversight over AI decisions.

6. Future Horizons

Jaguar Land Rover's success with AI in predictive maintenance is indicative of the broader potential for AI in manufacturing. As AI technology continues to evolve, we can expect to see its application in other areas of manufacturing, such as quality control, supply chain management, and even product design. This promises further innovations in efficiency, cost savings, and sustainability, heralding a new era in manufacturing.

AI in Customer Service: The Data Analytics Revolution at Starbucks

Starbucks, a global leader in the coffee industry, is improving the customer experience through the strategic use of data analytics and artificial intelligence (AI). By meticulously analysing customer data, Starbucks offers personalised recommendations and real-time notifications, significantly enhancing the customer experience. The linchpin of this transformation is the Deep Brew initiative, which utilises AI to optimise operations and personalise customer interactions.

1. The Objective

In the fiercely competitive coffee industry, delivering a unique and personalised customer experience is paramount. Starbucks sought to leverage its extensive customer data to not just meet, but exceed customer expectations, thereby fostering loyalty and enhancing satisfaction.

2. The AI Solution

Starbucks introduced Deep Brew, an AI-driven initiative aimed at revolutionising the brand's personalisation engine, labour allocations in stores, and inventory management. Deep Brew harnesses AI and IoT technologies to streamline operations while personalising the customer journey. It brings improvements in several key areas:

- **Personalised Customer Engagement**: By analysing previous orders and preferences, Starbucks offers tailored recommendations and engages customers with instant notifications about nearby stores or the availability of their favourite beverages.

- **Operational Efficiency**: Deep Brew AI is integrated into Starbucks' Mastrena super-automatic espresso machines, which are equipped with sensors for centralised logging and analysis of each espresso shot. Predictive analytics enable precision adjustments and preventative maintenance, enhancing machine performance and drink quality.

- **Enhanced Customer Support**: Starbucks employs social listening and generative AI to swiftly identify and address customer feedback. Immediate summarisation of responses enables prompt and effective customer service, greatly improving satisfaction levels.

3. Positive Outcomes and Impact

The deployment of AI and data analytics through Deep Brew has had a significant impact on Starbucks:

- **Personalisation**: Customers enjoy a more personalised service, fostering loyalty and encouraging repeat visits.

- **Operational Efficiency**: Improved labour allocations and inventory management lead to more efficient store operations and reduced waste.

- **Enhanced Customer Support**: Generative AI in customer service boosts agent productivity by 14% and lowers attrition by 9%, according to ServiceNow insights.

- **Predictive Maintenance**: Preventative maintenance on espresso machines ensures consistent quality and minimises downtime.

4. Overcoming Challenges

Implementing these AI innovations involved overcoming significant technical and logistical challenges, including the integration of volumetric capture technology and ensuring the AI-driven game intelligence authentically replicated real-world football strategies and dynamics.

5. Navigating Ethical Aspects

The application of AI and data analytics by Starbucks raises critical ethical considerations, especially concerning the privacy and security of customer data. Starbucks commits to managing customer information responsibly, ensuring all data-driven initiatives are transparent, consensual, and secure.

6. Future Horizons

Starbucks recognises the considerable potential in expanding the use of generative AI for customer service. The ongoing development of the Deep Brew initiative is set to further drive innovation in customer experience, operational efficiency, and personalised engagement.

Starbucks' strategic implementation of AI and data analytics exemplifies how technology can revolutionise the customer experience in retail, setting a new standard for personalised service and operational excellence.

AI in Human Resources: Unilever's Transformation

The integration of AI into human resources (HR) has brought about a revolution in HR practices, significantly enhancing the efficiency and fairness of recruitment, employee engagement, and performance management. A prime example of this modernisation is Unilever's adoption of AI for candidate screening in their recruitment process.

1. Setting The Goal

Unilever was faced with the dual challenges of managing a high volume of applicants from diverse backgrounds worldwide and ensuring a fair, unbiased recruitment process. Their goal was to address these challenges effectively.

2. The AI Solution

Unilever implemented an AI-driven recruitment process that includes digital applications, online games designed to evaluate various skills and traits, and video interviews analysed by AI for specific characteristics and expressions. This approach allows for a more objective assessment of candidates, focusing on potential, skills, and role suitability beyond just CVs or conventional assessment methods.

3. Positive Outcomes and Impact

The adoption of this AI-powered method has yielded notable benefits for Unilever:

- **Efficiency**: The recruitment timeline has been drastically shortened, with some positions filled in as little as 4 weeks, down from 4 months.

- **Diversity**: The process has enhanced the diversity of Unilever's hires by reducing the human biases inherent in traditional recruitment methods.

- **Candidate Experience**: The selection process has been perceived as more engaging and innovative by applicants, boosting Unilever's reputation as an employer.

4. Overcoming Challenges

Despite its successes, Unilever encountered obstacles such as ensuring AI's decision-making is explainable and unbiased, preserving a human element in HR processes, and protecting candidate data privacy.

5. Navigating Ethical Aspects

Unilever has tackled these challenges by integrating transparency into their AI-driven recruitment, offering feedback to candidates, and adhering to global data protection laws.

6. Future Horizons

The future of AI in HR is promising. We can anticipate advancements in:

- **Candidate Screening**: AI could assess a broader range of skills and predict potential performance.
- **Employee Engagement**: AI systems could monitor satisfaction and suggest morale-boosting actions.
- **Performance Management**: AI could provide unbiased assessments and suggest personalised training.

As AI evolves, its application could extend to workforce planning, talent management, and retention strategies. Unilever's use of AI in recruitment is a stepping stone towards a digital future in HR.

Footnotes

1) Learn more about how Google Health's AI help with diagnosing diabetic retinopathy here: https://health.google/caregivers/arda/

2) Learn more about how Revolut uses AI to prevent fraud here: https://techhq.com/2019/11/how-revoluts-sherlock-ai-saves-its-customers-from-fraud/

3) Learn more about predictive maintenance here: https://prophesy.eu/node/177

4) Learn more about Amazon's usage of AI in retail here: https://www.digitalcommerce360.com/2024/01/09/amazon-ai-improve-apparel-conversions/

5) Learn more about Unilever's usage of AI in the recruitment process here: https://aiexpert.network/case-study-revolutionizing-

6) Learn more about the usage of AI in EA Sports FC 24 here: https://www.ea.com/games/ea-sports-fc/news/fc-24-gameplay-deepdive

7) Learn more about Starbuck's Deep Brew here: https://www.linkedin.com/pulse/starbucks-magic-artificial-intelligence-enhancing-coffee-pavithra-s/

Conclusion

As we embarked on the creation of this book, our intention was to guide you through the multifaceted world of artificial intelligence (AI) in a manner that demystifies its complexities and highlights its potential for societal good. By meticulously selecting and answering the most pertinent 100 AI questions, we aimed to ease readers into the AI landscape, making the vast and sometimes intimidating field of AI accessible and engaging. The inclusion of a comprehensive AI Glossary further served to illuminate the main areas of AI, providing clarity on key terms and concepts that form the backbone of AI discussions and applications. Moreover, through the presentation of 106 real-world examples, our goal was to demonstrate the pervasive and positive impact of AI across various sectors, showcasing how AI technologies are already enhancing our world in significant ways.

This journey through the book has revealed the depth and breadth of AI's influence, from improving healthcare outcomes and driving financial innovation to revolutionising customer service and reshaping the future of work. Each section, each case study, was chosen not only for its educational value but also to inspire a sense of optimism and possibility about what can be achieved when humans and machines collaborate. These stories of innovation and transformation across industries like healthcare, finance, retail, gaming, manufacturing, and human resources underline a critical message: AI is not a force of displacement but a catalyst for augmentation and enhancement of human capabilities.

As we stand in 2024, on the brink of a new era of business transformation powered by AI, it's clear that our actions today will significantly influence the shape of tomorrow. This era, marked by rapid advancements and the integration of AI into every aspect of our lives, calls for a thoughtful examination of both the opportunities and challenges that lie ahead. It is our hope that this book has equipped you with a clearer understanding of AI's potential and provided a roadmap for harnessing AI in your work and beyond.

The responsible application of AI, coupled with a relentless reimagining of work, holds the key to unlocking the benefits of AI for all. It's a journey that requires both caution and courage, as we navigate the ethical implications and strive for innovations that enhance rather than diminish our shared human experience. The future of AI is not a distant dream but a present reality, and it's up to us to shape it in a way that reflects our highest aspirations for society.

In closing, let us embrace the future with open arms, recognising that the era of AI presents unparalleled opportunities for growth, innovation, and progress. The future is indeed here, and through collaborative effort, thoughtful application, and a commitment to ethical principles, we can all be part of a movement that leverages AI for the greater good. Let this book be a starting point for a journey that continues well beyond its pages, inspiring action, conversation, and continuous learning in the exciting and evolving world of AI. The path ahead is rich with potential—let's step forward together, ready to make the most of the AI-enabled future that awaits.

About the Author

Mark Kelly is Co-Founder of an international AI Staffing firm and Founder of AI Ireland. Over his career, he has worked with hundreds of business and government leaders around the globe, providing workforce solutions. He has been instrumental in bringing together the AI community in Ireland and showcasing how AI can be used to solve business and societal challenges.

Kelly studied business studies at TUI and completed a Masters in Business in UCD Smurfit Business School. In 2018 over a coffee he delved into the world of AI and he was hooked, and this led to a career-long pursuit of interviewing leaders of AI.

A frequent speaker and writer on AI applied to industry and technology issues, Kelly has been featured in a variety of media outlets, including The Sunday Times, The Irish Times, The Irish Independent, RTE News Network and Newstalk 106.

Kelly is passionate advocate for AI for good and created the AI Awards in 2018 where over 500 applications of AI have been shared on the island of Ireland. Mark and his family live in Dublin, Ireland.

Appendix A. Further Sources of Information

Further Reading and Resources

As we conclude "AI Unleashed Essentials: The AI-Driven Leader's Quick Reference," it's evident that the exploration of Artificial Intelligence (AI) is a journey that extends far beyond the final pages of this book. To facilitate your continued exploration and deeper engagement with AI, I recommend several resources and avenues for further learning.

AI Unleashed: Navigating the AI Revolution as a Business Executive

For readers who have valued the insights and practical guidance provided herein, my preceding publication, "AI Unleashed: Navigating the AI Revolution as a Business Executive," delves deeper into the strategic application of AI within the business landscape. This book is designed to equip executives with the insights needed to navigate the complexities of AI, ensuring successful leadership in an era of technological transformation. "AI Unleashed" is available for purchase on Amazon UK at [here](https://www.amazon.co.uk/Unleashed-Navigating-Revolution-Demystifying-Intelligence-ebook/dp/B0CK7RKWMR), serving as an essential resource for those looking to further their strategic understanding of AI.

AI Ireland Website and Podcast

AI Ireland plays a crucial role in promoting the adoption and understanding of AI across various sectors in Ireland. I encourage you to visit the AI Ireland website at [www.aiireland.ie] and AI Awards website (http://www.aiawards.ie), a central hub for AI-related resources, news, and events that can enrich your understanding and practical application of AI technologies.

Additionally, the AI Ireland Podcast features enlightening conversations with leading AI experts, offering deep dives into the latest developments, ethical considerations, and practical uses of AI. These discussions will keep you abreast of the cutting edge in AI research and industry practices.

Book Mark Kelly as an AI Speaker

Engaging with AI thought leadership in a live setting can profoundly impact your understanding and strategic thinking regarding AI. As an experienced AI speaker, Kelly offers consultancy for businesses, keynote speeches for conferences, and workshops for educational institutions, providing tailored insights to meet your specific challenges and opportunities. Booking a speaking engagement offers a unique opportunity for direct interaction, helping to clarify complex AI concepts and identify strategic opportunities for its application within your organisation.

Engage Further with AI:

- **Read "AI Unleashed":** Enhance your strategic grasp of AI by incorporating "AI Unleashed" into your reading list, an invaluable companion for business leaders navigating the AI landscape.

- **Explore AI Ireland:** Visit [AI Ireland] (http://www.aiireland.ie) and subscribe to the AI Ireland Podcast for continuous updates and insights into the AI ecosystem.

- **Consultancy and Speaking Engagements:** Consider booking a consultancy session or speaking engagement to explore AI's strategic applications tailored to your organisational needs.

Index

Made in United States
Troutdale, OR
03/20/2024

18600518R00136